Twenty-First-Century Management

Twenty-First-Century Management

The Revolutionary Strategies
That Have Made
Computer Associates
a Multibillion-Dollar Software Giant

Hesh Kestin

THE ATLANTIC MONTHLY PRESS
NEW YORK

TO THE PEOPLE OF CA, WITHOUT
WHOSE GENEROSITY OF TIME AND SPIRIT
THIS BOOK COULD NOT HAVE BEEN WRITTEN

Published simultaneously in Canada
Printed in the United States of America

Library of Congress Cataloging-in-Publication Data

Kestin, Hesh.
Twenty-first-century management: the revolutionary strategies that have made Computer Associates a multibillion-dollar software giant / by Hesh Kestin.
Includes bibliographical references.
ISBN 0-87113-524-8
1. Computer Associates International. 2. Computer software industry—United States—Management—Case studies. I. Title.
HD9696.C64C634   1992   004'.068—dc20   92-4089

Design by Laura Hough

The Atlantic Monthly Press
19 Union Square West
New York, NY 10003

First printing

Contents

Preface

Several years back, when I was European correspondent for *Forbes*, I found myself looking at American business practice from afar. This enforced perspective shocked me into a rather delayed recognition of the mess that U.S. business had become.

Like most Americans, I had it in my head that the United States was the ranking world expert on doing business, with the best techniques, the best people, and as a result, the best track record. But as I traveled and spent time with the leaders of European industry, I began to get the feeling that measuring business performance by the historical record was a little like putting money on a horse based only on its turf history as limned in the racing papers. After all, what makes the past the past is that, beyond any contradiction, it is over. I found myself growing skeptical about American business skills—in the same way I'd think twice about putting fifty bucks on a favorite that was now marching around the paddock with an obvious limp. Was American business management still good? If so, why did a major by-product of U.S. business seem to be business books?

There was something surreal about it all. The day Lee Iacocca's book came out, Chrysler was hemorrhaging red ink and certainly would have drowned in it long before, were it not for the kind of massive federal bailout that has given the world the Lada, the former Soviet Union's best-selling family car. Yet readers—supposedly hardheaded business people—

flocked to buy Iacocca's book. Was it because *Iacocca* is an acronym for "I am chairman of Chrysler Corporation of America"? If so, the coincidence is no more illuminating than was the book.

As the economy wound down and more and more businesses failed or were acquired like gambling chips, more and more books appeared on the shelves. In *The Wall Street Journal*, ads appeared each day heralding new and dramatic breakthroughs in business thinking: *The One-Minute Manager* (what was this—the manager as soft-boiled egg?), *In Search of Quality, In Search of Excellence, In Search of Competitiveness, Business Strategies for the Nineties, New Wave Business, Permanent Wave Business*, and a whole silly lot more. Between 1980 and 1990, U.S. publishers sold millions of copies of thousands of business titles, a varied lot not only in quality and excellence but in subject and approach.

All had in common the premise that by doing this and such and, at all costs—which was often the result—avoiding that, a business manager could solve all his problems without resorting to gunplay and get home in time to see his stock price leave FNN's television screen and start climbing the wallpaper.

By the end of the decade the market for business books seemed to be dominated by two groups: (1) computer-armed academics who had spent their lives studying market conditions and had the printouts to prove conclusively that garbage in still means garbage out; (2) Japanese soothsayers—or their fans—weighing in with good advice if you happen to be Japanese, have the government in Tokyo behind you to cut out foreign competition, and employ docile zombies who smile through eleven-hour workdays, execrable pay, and zero job satisfaction before going home to apartments the size of your standard American golf cart.

Meanwhile, on the home front the U.S. automobile industry—once the flag bearer of an economy that didn't need business books—continued to shrivel as a process of bureaucratic symbiosis that would have felt right at home in Tagliotti, home of the Lada, kept bringing poor products to market. If in 1980 it was difficult to find consumer electronics—TVs, music systems, microwaves—marked "Made in the U.S.A.," by the close of the decade it was difficult to conceive they could be.

Faced with this failure, people who had managed that very morning to tie their own shoelaces could be spotted in public mumbling about the coming of the service economy, a kind of theme park in which accountants would buy their hamburgers at McDonald's from personable burger flippers who would all grow up to be accountants.

Like any elegant but ultimately unbuildable perpetual motion machine or some national Ponzi scheme, nothing would be produced but a monumental mutual back scratch. Alas, amid the back scratching few considered that we might have to actually produce something. This complicated matters no end.

Whatever the ultimate truth about the reason for America's rise to economic dominance between the World Wars—yes, only that recently—clearly something was amiss. Perhaps, then, our salvation lay in careful analysis of times when things were far better, or at least less amiss. Why had we once been dominant?

There were those who pointed to the Protestant ethic, but there were also those who said it had something to do with the waves of immigrants, mostly Catholics and Jews, who sparked each decade with their hunger and desire. Those taking the long view fell into two camps. Some attributed America's late-lamented economic brilliance to its wealth of natural resources (more abundant than Canada's and far less abundant than Brazil's) and its system of rivers, highways, and railroads (far less extensive than Europe's). Then there were the fatalists, who as much as compared a nation's economic vitality to a man's strength or a woman's ability to bring forth child. In their eyes it was all a global footrace: the Greeks overtaking the Romans, whose lead passed in quick succession to the Arabs, the Iberians, the Brits, and finally the Yanks, who were in the midst of handing it over to the Japanese, who themselves had the Taiwanese at their heels, followed by the Koreans coming up fast at the quarter turn. Where, one wondered, were the Eskimos?

As I traveled around Europe for *Forbes*, however, it was clear that this kind of fatalism was merely a failure of will with a medical excuse. If the United States was on its way to becoming an industrial desert, business flowers of all kinds and under many conditions were blooming all over the continent and even further afield.

In France, for instance, I was privileged to spend time in the mountains of Savoy with Georges Salomon. He had built an innovative ski company based on a kind of mystical belief in better ways to do things—from design (his seemed predicated on such unsubstantive hunches that the very idea would be laughed out of venture capitalism school) to manufacturing approach (that combined robots with human labor in a kind of craftsman's assembly line).

In Zurich, I spent a long and fascinating day with Robert Staubli and Martin Junger, who were then, respectively, president and chief financial officer of the world's best airline. Several years later I discovered that both had been terribly embarrassed by the wine served in the five-star restaurant that is the company's executive dining room—it had tasted of cork, which any Swiss oenophile would have noticed right away. But I was too busy trying to figure out how Swissair could remain so consistently profitable while providing such a high level of expensive service. As an international journalist, I had found myself passing up other airlines to fly Swissair even if it meant taking a less direct route. In a time of serious problems for U.S. carriers—a crisis far from over—here was an airline that had institutionalized success. The answer was only partially revealed when Junger delightedly lifted the cushion off Staubli's office couch to demonstrate the lengths the company would go to hide tremendous reserves of cash. (There was no cash under the cushions—it was all hidden in Swiss bookkeeping.) When Junger drove me back to my hotel, it occurred to me that in the United States, where the mere mention of *Forbes* is enough to get whole divisions of corporate flacks jabbering at you into the phone, no chief financial officer of a $30 billion company would drive a Swiss journalist to his hotel. Yet here in Switzerland, where *Forbes* was not terribly well-known, it had become very important for the top kicks of the world's most successful airline to make sure I understood how it was done.

In Israel I ran into a fellow named David Sinigaglia, who ran the daughter company of a U.S. electronics outfit called North Hills. David had done well in business in England and the United States, but in Israel he had accomplished the impossible by smashing through the barrier between management and labor that was at least part of the reason the world's most talent-filled state is possessor of one of the world's most problem-filled economies. A few years later, when a U.S. company named Porta Systems acquired North Hills, Sinigaglia was put in charge of mother and daughter companies both. Was the acquisition's target the U.S. company or its foreign subsidiary?

In Denmark I visited Lego, a family firm then quietly selling some $2 billion a year in toys of such rudimentary design their basic patents were no longer in force. Yet the company's genius at marketing prevented knockoffs from making a dent in Lego sales; an American attempt to copy and sell at cut price the company's distinctive interlocking plastic bricks went the way of a similar try by the Taiwanese.

By the time I returned to the United States in 1990, I had concluded that at least part of America's problem was tied to the phenomenon of the business books themselves. So long hidebound in the mindless and often shabbily vain pursuit of its own perfection, American industry was simply looking for a quick fix, a new formula that would replace the old and which, like the old, could be embraced until death. Would American business, like the dinosaurs, perfect itself right out of a job?

I didn't know. But rather abruptly I did realize that what had attracted me to European business (most of which is quite as mindlessly self-corrupted as that in the States) was its plentiful supply of new models. I too had been guilty of looking for the quick fix.

But the quick fix just didn't make sense, and still doesn't, because even the most innovative and visionary model, once it is set in corporate concrete, contains the neatly built-in germ of its own eventual destruction. That is for sure, because the world's rate of change is such that any model will soon be obsolete; the more authoritative the model, the quicker its demise.

Would we forever be stuck with building models only to see them succeeded by newer ones? There was something in this of slash-and-burn, that most primitive example of the world's first industry, agriculture. We were doing the same thing, endlessly clearing patches of jungle and then abandoning these fields when the soil played out. It seemed as unpromising as built-in obsolescence, stockings made to run, cars made to break down, factories built to rusty abandonment, business books.

Thus armed with hopelessness, I had lunch one day in Boston with George Gendron, editor of *Inc.*, who had turned his monthly magazine into a kind of relentless Baedeker of the best and worst you'd ever want to know about new and growing companies. Around dessert I mentioned Computer Associates and wondered if its size, with revenues then approaching $1.4 billion, meant it would not be of interest to *Inc.*'s readership of more modest entrepreneurs. "Oh," George said, "that's the one that's grown by acquisition."

"Acquisition?" I replied.

Immediately it became clear to both of us that we were talking about two very different companies—one that was so weak it needed to feed on other firms, the other one so strong it had been able to absorb them successfully and not, in the process, choke. Rather more absorbed with our own digestive systems, we swirled this around for a while like the wine in the bottom of our glasses but concluded nought. On the shuttle flight back to New York, I realized what was wrong: I knew nothing about the company.

Surprisingly little had been written about CA, I was to learn, and much of that leaned heavily on what, after reading all of it, I came to think of as the Subgum School of business journalism: "Chinese Immigrant Makes Good (Endlessly)." Obviously my fellow hacks had fallen back on that because they could not figure out how a company this badly run could make so much money. I did a chart of CA's growth. It looked like a cutaway of one half of the Eiffel Tower—85 degrees up and fifteen years long. If this was the second-fastest-growing mature company in America, I didn't know the first.

But it was no model for American industry, and nobody

Computer Associates International, Inc.

REVENUES

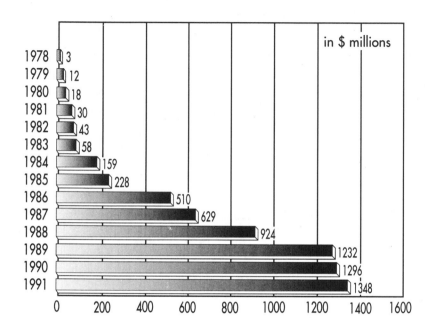

Year	Revenue (in $ millions)
1978	3
1979	12
1980	18
1981	30
1982	43
1983	58
1984	159
1985	228
1986	510
1987	629
1988	924
1989	1232
1990	1296
1991	1348

would ever write a business book about it. Its chairman ran CA like a storefront family business. It was so rife with nepotism that a shockingly large proportion of its nearly eight thousand employees could name at least one co-worker who was related by either blood or longtime friendship. Operationally there were no rules, or they kept changing. Nobody ever bothered writing a memo to let others know what he or she was doing. Lines of authority shifted constantly, usually undermined by CA's chairman himself or his brother, president of the company.

Employee turnover was thought to be the highest in the software industry, which may itself have the highest turnover of all U.S. businesses. Understandable, since CA evidently thought so little of its labor force that it paid bottom dollar for its office space and furnishings. You could count the employee benefits on the fingers of a hand that had survived a serious industrial accident: a health club and free breakfast, but that was probably only because CA chairman Charles B. Wang liked to play basketball and eat donuts.

In fact, Wang seemed to run the company by whim, so that at least once a year he would reorganize it from top to bottom. The rumor was he did it every month. By himself. Just like that.

With the idea of writing a magazine article on what had to be the business world's longest-running lucky streak, I came to CA for a week. I stayed the better part of a year. What I found was a company so revolutionary that it had put aside the dusty principles of American business totalitarianism and laughed off all the new panaceas.

CA's formula was so simple it seemed ridiculous. But what seems all the more ridiculous is that I, supremely cynical about business books and their claim to having all the right answers, have now written one.

Well, this book has no right answers, only a lot of questioning. It details no plan, only an emerging process. It found nothing set in concrete, only the perpetual elasticity of such relentless self-renewal that even those within CA were too busily involved in it to be aware of what it was.

"It's just good people," Charles Wang told me at our first meeting. I thought he was being disingenuous. He wasn't. It is. They are. And this is the story of how they got that way.

How to Read This Book

This is a business book with few numbers, some lonely and not very sophisticated charts, and zero rules and regulations for better business management. And considering that it is a book about the world's leading independent vendor and developer of software, there is little if anything about CA software. For all practical purposes *Twenty-First-Century Management* could be about a company that irradiates guano.

This is also not the book that will finally explain what the hell software is and how it is developed and sold. Nor will it go into the private lives of CA's corporate officers and their subcorporate cats and dogs—it is not an exposé.

It may well be the only business book around that's full of people talking.

In that sense it is a business book the way *Moby-Dick* is the definitive guide to marine mammals. There is whaling in that book, but I wouldn't suggest holding it open with your left hand while grasping a harpoon with your right. Though Melville wrote from deep within a company—it was in fact a ship's company—his tale is not prescriptive ("Twenty-seven Rules for Hunting and Catching a White Whale"). It is passionate. It describes a quest.

This does not mean the reader should be sentenced to a quest of his own. To quote Sheldon Zalaznick, former managing editor at *Forbes* and a man for whom short *is* sweet: "Just give us the cream, Hesh." Shelley had sympathy for the civilian. Simply because a journalist was proud of having collected mountains of numbers and toxic waste dumps full of data, that was no reason to drop this detritus on the reader. This is usually a person intent on catching an airplane, not a whale.

Which is why this book is neither long nor complicated, neither technical nor particularly high-flown. In what may be fitting tribute to a company that has replaced the seventy-five-page memo with a chat in the hallway, *Twenty-First-Century Management* employs a narrative line (in boldface type) that can be read quickly as it threads through personal commentary (in normal type) by the real human beings who make up CA.

If this reinvents the business book, there is an advantage. The reader can deal with it on his own terms. Think of it as a superhighway you can get off of anytime to explore an attractive back road. Or read it straight through. Either way, know that there is a disadvantage as well. A business book your kids can understand is going to cause them to wonder what's so damn hard about what you do all day.

Part One:

Evolution

I. Context

For an industrial giant, invisibility is not easy to come by, but Computer Associates International, Inc., has just about managed to pull it off.

One would think a company that broke the $1 billion revenue mark after little more than a decade and that now, three years later in the midst of a serious recession, is closing in on twice that would be pointed out with boring regularity as a rare and inspiring American triumph, with the State Department practically running guided tours and the news magazines pestering CA founder and chairman Charles B. Wang for authoritative answers to the usual dumb questions about the ongoing crisis in the economy, how to stop Sony from taking over the world, and why Johnny not only can't read but can't count.

In an era in which Japan has all but given the boot to American technological leadership, it seems only reasonable that a corporation whose subsidiaries in Europe are the largest independent software companies in their respective countries would be talked about constantly as an example of successful American multinationalism.

Here is a company that has brought to market more products than any software company in the world, a company that continues to develop commercial programs with a speed and efficiency that gives the lie to the conventional wisdom that good

3

software requires many years of development with many hundreds of programmers working in cadres like so many mindless techno-ants.

And this is a corporation that, since its inception as a four-person software outfit selling one program, has acquired and integrated unto itself no fewer than forty-two companies at a cost of some $2 billion, a corporate entity so revolutionary in its management and so successful in nearly every aspect of its being that one would think it would be at least as well-known and admired as IBM or Digital Equipment Corp. (DEC) or Microsoft or Lotus or Campbell's soup.

One would think so. And one would be wrong.

Indeed, in computer circles as on Wall Street, there remains an odd unwillingness to face the fact that CA exists, much less that it should be admired. A good deal of this has to do with CA's product, which in its many permutations always comes down to software that has all the inherent sex appeal of the gas turbine or the machine tool. In the main, CA's clients are corporations dependent on high-powered mainframe computing and the million-dollar software budgets that support it. CA's raison d'etre is to provide software that permits IBM, DEC, and other hardware to produce more and better work so that their corporate operators can avoid even heavier investments in more computing machinery. This strategy has not endeared CA to IBM, whose tens of thousands of programmers seem purposely to produce such inefficient software that the only solution to greater client needs is more clunky IBM computers rather than systems to declunk them. Students, journalists, small-business people—in short, the sort of human beings who buy their own

4

socks—are unlikely ever to have heard of a CA product, much less to have bought one. Less than 20 percent of CA revenues derive from desktop software. Microsoft, with which CA is now neck and neck in the race for who sells more software, is far better known because it sells its few inexpensive products to millions.*

CA sells products priced in the thousands, the hundreds of thousands, and the millions, but to far fewer clients. Had the two gone into communications and not computing, CA would be making enormous and extremely complex switching systems to run entire telephone companies, Microsoft would be making cute little phones that light up in the dark.

To be sure, were CA as aggressive about its public image as it is about its products, it would be a household name the way IBM was even before it sold its first personal computer to a private, noncorporate personal human being. While CA advertises heavily in the information processing press, it advertises almost not at all in the general business press and absolutely zero in places like *Time* and *Newsweek*, where private citizens are likely to form an impression that something has poked itself over the print horizon and so, *ipso facto*, exists. When it does advertise, CA is generally pushing specific products, not CA as an institu-

---

*Financial comparison of the two giants is an accounting minefield. Microsoft appeared to have pulled ahead in revenues as of 1991, but this included $213 million from sales of hardware. Subtracting the hardware revenues leaves $1.63 billion net. By the same measure and for approximately the same period, CA has characteristically understated its total revenues by choosing not to take into account at least $348 million from companies acquired for cash in 1991. With these included, CA revenues surpassed $1.7 billion.

tion. Unlike IBM, it rarely does corporate advertising, does not promote its name, does not promote its image and, as a consequence, has none. The odd result is that while IBM continues to be admired as a paragon of corporate success, even as it hurries to reconstruct before it simply collapses, CA, which reorganizes itself top to bottom every year but never talks about it, remains unknown.

Alone among publically traded U.S. companies, CA does not have a corporate public relations department. But what ultimately underpins CA's invisibility is that few with any stake in American industry—not in the corporate world, not on Wall Street, not in the business schools—have been prepared to deal with the issues its success has raised. CA is invisible because, like history's losing generals, the leaders of corporate America have remained crouched behind their own Maginot Line, unwilling to admit that the face of war has changed.

This is not objective invisibility—it is subjective. CA is not seen largely because it makes people in the business world very uncomfortable to see it.

Corporate America's Maginot Line will not hold any better than the original did. (The Maginot metaphor, as it turns out, is one with a lineage that predates the Maginot itself: when a thin and strung-out defense very similar to the Maginot was suggested to Napoleon a century before the building of the line, he is said to have asked, "What are you trying to do—prevent smuggling?")

Whether ahead of its time or simply out of sync with it, CA as a corporation—and as a collection of human beings—has been suffering for years from aggravated outsider syndrome: a rare corporate disease normally familiar to high school students who have transferred in from out of town and become invisible in the halls.

What makes this all the more absurd is that the outsider is now clearly the industry leader. Ignoring this reality is a bit like pretending the aggressive little pussycat over there is not a tiger cub and keeping up the pretense even after it is fully grown. Ignoring the future when it stands there and invites you to lunch is to pass up sharing lunch for being it.

Yet on first look what Charles Wang has done with CA is merely to have demonstrated a driven marketing brilliance that is served by an uncommon parallel mastery on the technological side. This is hardly unique. Before and after such giants as Thomas Edison, Henry Ford, and Tom Watson, lesser examples of the type have sprouted every year in their hundreds, if not thousands, from what seems to be an especially fertile American soil. This sort of techno-marketing genius would have brought Charles modest success no matter what, but it is not the factor that has powered CA to absolute dominance in the kind of software that provides the key to communications and control in the data centers of nearly all the companies on the Forbes and Fortune 500 lists, together with government agencies both here and abroad. And certainly it is not what has created CA's unique position of being an outsider in the industry it leads.

The single phrase that best describes that industry's response to CA's success is "resentment fueled by fear." Simply put, CA's success is a challenge to the received orthodoxy of American business, upon which methodology CA has turned its corporate back. People who do things the accepted way don't happen to love that.

In many instances they love it so little that they're willing to continue· to fail rather than learn from CA. To switch but not fundamentally alter our military metaphor: like the precisely instructed and well-drilled Redcoats who were unable to stop losing according to the book, orthodox American businesses are not going to scrap their gloriously traditional way of doing things just to fight an army of innovating Colonials. People at CA remain amazed, for instance, that other companies have for sixteen years not followed its lead on flexible pricing arrangements.

From CA's own inception as a company with no cash—it bartered programming talent for its first office space—Charles understood that everyone was, to one extent or another, in the same boat. To bring in business, he established so many payment options for CA software that sales became a cointoss that, assuming ballpark similarity in product pricing and quality from one company to the next, always had to come up heads. Today there is practically no fair way a client cannot pay for CA software. Payment options are often suggested by the clients themselves.

Make sense? Yes, but only if CA as an operating company is so flexible that new payment options can be approved simply and efficiently. In most companies, pricing—never mind alternative methods of payment—is established by committee. Arnold S. Mazur, now CA's executive vice president of sales, took charge of what had been Applied Data Research (ADR) when CA took it over in 1988, and immediately set about reorganizing ADR's pricing structure. When word got out, an ADR vice president hurried in to say it couldn't be done—ADR's pricing committee hadn't met yet.

Poor CA, it didn't have a pricing committee. Instead, it was compelled to limp along relying on one man with a sharpened pencil. This single individual has the power to set up a price structure and the same power to alter it when a client comes in and says he wants to pay 15 percent down in U.S. currency, with the rest over three years in 40 percent dollars and 60 percent a mixed basket of Portuguese escudos, Italian lire, and Belgian francs—and would it be possible to package the software with another program and pay for that at a 20 percent discount (though the discount does not normally apply to the second program), but beginning 180 days after installation and payable entirely in Swiss francs indexed to today's dollar–franc rate so long as the spread between the current and later rates does not exceed 10 percent?

That CA can make this kind of arrangement is a function of the way it operates. There are no committees at CA—no committees at all. If there were, Computer Associates would be as sclerotic as the companies that yell "No fair!" when CA gets the business. For these companies to follow CA's lead on pricing and payment options would be to ask the same companies to get rid of their pricing committees. The next step would be getting rid of the whole rigid hierarchy of stratified layabouts, a decision unlikely to be taken by a committee of said stratified layabouts. Is it any wonder that companies with etched-in-stone pricing arrangements—in fact, with etched-in-stone everything—do not like CA? IBM, arguably the greatest single business success story of our time, a standard-bearer of order, structure, and hierarchy that by anyone's reckoning has long been the model twentieth-century company, is nobody's model (not even IBM's) for the twenty-first.

As with any company, the character of the leadership is father to the culture further down. While top and bottom are—as we shall see—awesomely inappropriate terms for the way CA is set up, the principle holds. For instance, because of the aggressive flexibility of its corporate leadership, CA salespeople are probably the most competent, well-trained, and driven in the business. Though this book is not about CA sales techniques, much of which is proprietary, certainly the kind of people CA fields is yet another reason it is not loved, both because of the way they work—think of the U.S. Marines armed with order books—and, to an extent unknown, who they are.

Perhaps because Charles Wang is an immigrant himself (he came to the United States from China as a child), he has had an open mind about the kind of people hired to represent his company. While most firms dealing with corporate America at the boardroom level make it a point to choose button-down male WASPs armed with M.B.A.'s from good schools, CA has delighted in discovering people who could understand software and sell it: black, yellow, white, or anything else. For years its number one salesperson was that high-echelon boardroom rarity, a woman: Anita Lum not only had a degree from an unimpressive city college but had not even finished CA's own training course. Not only is she Chinese, but she has the shadow of an accent. She does bring to her job a certain do-or-die quality, but then she has an advantage over white male Harvard M.B.A.'s: few of those graduated from the Cultural Revolution as full-fledged Red Guards.

CA salespeople quickly built a reputation for zealotry. Along with most of CA, you were either a zealot or out the door. In one bizarre instance, CA discovered that a star salesman so psyched himself up to come away with something tangible from his sales calls that he never left an office without slipping something into his pocket—a ballpoint pen, a sheet of paper, a paper clip, anything. He would not leave without something. His managers discovered it because he would do the same thing when visiting CA headquarters.

This may say something about the kind of people drawn to work for CA, but it says even more about the kind of company that draws them. Sure, CA salespeople, like CA people in every department, are well rewarded, but something else is driving them. In Italy, where CA runs the country's biggest software company, the managing director, Ettore Petrini, routinely divides his sales force into two teams: the team that produces less each month earns the privilege of shining the shoes of the team that produces more. (In summer they wash the winning team's cars; for an Italian this is only slightly less demeaning.)

IBM may be reorganizing, and it will be reorganizing for years, but it will never reorganize down to the shoeshine level. To say that the corporate culture is different is to say nothing at all; to say the entire character of the companies is different is merely to approach the truth. The species is different. People at IBM or any other computer-industry company—hell, any other company—who are making $200,000 a year do not shine their own shoes, much less someone else's.

CA is often criticized as cheap. And in one way it is, far cheaper than can be imagined. While it pays its employees better than other software companies, CA is not the kind of place where you get a decorating budget for your office, not least because senior managers don't always have offices but seem to be perfectly capable of making major decisions behind a flimsy partition that may have been acquired secondhand. Not only is there no fleet of corporate aircraft—remarkable in a company with sixty-seven offices across the United States and sixty-three more around the world—but CA has never so much as chartered a plane. Regardless of position, everyone flies scheduled; the preferred class is coach. Even coach looks good next to CA's offices, which are stocked with the best buys in off-the-shelf plastic, fiberboard, and sheetmetal; the day someone invents paper furniture, CA will snap it up. Though he is now among the best-paid company chairmen in America, Charles Wang still uses the plywood desk he refinished himself when the company began in bartered office space. In CA's spanking-new corporate headquarters at Islandia, New York, none of the furniture is new.

Managers of corporations with endless layers of fatty perks and marblings of status symbols do not adore this kind of thing. And they're right not to. CA is a direct threat to what is widely held to be truth ("I make the decisions"), justice ("So my desk has to be solid gold"), and what's become the American way ("Suck up to me long enough, and you'll get one too"). This rewards virtue, but it is the wrong virtue. Neither patience nor sycophancy is going to get decisions made and things done. The price of a hierarchy of perks comes out of the pockets of those who should be rewarded and usually aren't—those who pull, not those who ride.

Consider this story, probably apocryphal, that still circulates around CA: An aggressive middle manager (at another company) has his raincoat stolen at the end of a sixteen-hour day while visiting a branch office abroad during a legal holiday in the United States, a day when everyone else in his office is relaxing at home. After returning with the problems in the branch office sorted out and a million dollars' worth of new business in his briefcase, he routinely makes out his expense report and adds the cost of a new raincoat. But the item is disapproved, struck off by accounting. Flash forward to the next month: our manager is no longer straining to solve problems in geographically inconvenient branch offices; nor does he bring in any more new business than he must. And when he does file his next regular expense report, this line is added in parentheses under his signature: "P.S.: See if you can find the raincoat."

Few of us will not take pleasure in this story. Most people have been screwed by the very corporations for which they have been asked to sacrifice their all. The only thing more galling than good work unrewarded is seeing shoddy work rewarded only too generously, as worthless managers who make the right corporate noises rise well past their levels of competency into a kind of wing-tipped nirvana in which all corporate errors are by definition made by some fool several levels down. What is not normally understood is the subtle connection between these two situations: if you look closely, the worthless managers are wearing our raincoats.

This is because an equitable situation in which people are rewarded has its price, and it is high. There just is not enough money around to pay for performance while maintaining a nonperforming hierarchy in the style to which it has become accustomed. Alas, if you want the one, you've got to ax the other. This kind of hard-edged thinking has not endeared CA to the very people who run most American corporations—and could run them better. As La Rochefoucauld put it, "There is nothing so distasteful as the lesson of a good example."

How distasteful, then, it must be for a company like Ameritech, which sold off a money loser like ADR only to watch CA immediately cut out unproductive managers and their even less productive perks—and in so doing pay off the $170 million purchase price not in five years' worth of revenues but in five months'. To say that CA had some magic formula is to seriously underestimate the simple rationality of people who are able to discern that heavy fixed overheads do not add to revenues and that when you have healthy revenues and are still broke, you don't have to look far for why. ADR's director of marketing and its entire sales force were actually getting bonuses while the company was seriously in the red. Everyone was getting bonuses. How come? Because this veteran company—the furthest thing from a start-up situation (in which it is understood revenues will not cover costs)—was simply budgeting for a loss. Hey, they were losing less than they had expected, right? Right. That's worth a bonus, right?

Wrong. By cutting out the dead wood and rewarding those who were actually working, CA was able to start ADR's turnaround in the time it takes a speed-reader to zip through this book. How pleasant it must have been for the really good people at ADR, who had suffered for so long under a management that was, in both senses of the term, out to lunch—and no less unpleasant for that management. Between throwing out the lemons and concentrating such administrative functions as accounting at CA headquarters, 50 percent of ADR's payroll was suddenly able to produce the same 100 percent of revenues and then some. With the former ADR paying for itself, CA was able to concentrate on using the acquired products to supply desirable components for existing CA programs, which themselves may then augment and improve the acquired products. Meanwhile, CA developers and marketers and those in the acquired company—by now something of a misnomer, because once acquired it becomes CA, not a subsidiary, not a division, but just CA—are able to work together on new products. For every product CA has acquired, the company has developed and brought to market at least one completely new one.

Because CA is in the main interested only in companies with legitimate products and strong sales, the ADR tale is hardly a novelty. The same story has been repeated dozens of times in large companies acquired for hundreds of millions each—like Uccel, Cullinet, On-Line, and Pansophic—and small ones with one product generated by technical sophistication, but without a clue as to what to do with it. Reviewing these acquisitions is like fast-forwarding through a collection of early television westerns in which an outsider is called in to bring justice to a town under seige from its own corrupt leadership. After a while you wonder that no one ever complained that it is all the same plot, sometimes even the same lines.

So when Wall Street analysts question CA's ability to absorb and turn around money-losing companies, they're right. But only based on their own limited understanding. Like their colleagues in the consulting business—one individual at a major computer-industry consultancy still questions CA's ability to develop a product it has been successfully selling for years—the analysts are so unimpressed with this miracle that shouldn't be that they're willing to ignore it. Wall Street is not interested in management brilliance based on dead-simple ideas it would prefer not to know about. In an age of industrial sophistry, Wall Street will always turn its back on what it cannot understand, much less explain, and cheer instead any company with a great little product, half computer terminal and half chili dog, say, or a cure for cancer based on a biogenetic patent derived from shark spit. Now that's sexy.

Wall Street can sell that, and would rather, because good management means only steady long-term growth, which means you aren't swapping today's bionic chili dog for tomorrow's shark spit—which means no commissions.

Whether this analysis does or does not go too far—it doesn't—one thing sexy isn't is a CA manager who might be a woman or a minority or an immigrant from some country where the citizenry is rumored to cook M.B.A.'s in big pots, someone who not only likes to make decisions but is encouraged to do so and then is rewarded or punished accordingly. In fact, it not only is not sexy, it's anything from a damned unpleasant idea (when it's just vaguely out there) to an indirect threat (when CA is about to acquire a company you thought was well-run because it is run like yours) to eviscerating (when the acquired company is yours).

Though your slow-to-average blindfolded puppy can easily appreciate the dynamics of such a takeover, the perception in the acquired company, or in companies fearful of being acquired, is something else. Here is a fat, morbidly sclerotic, money-losing company on the verge of bankruptcy about to be taken over by a slim, dynamic, money-making company. What to do? Why, blame the acquirer, of course. Blame it for being cheap (it sounds better than cost efficient), blame it for being cutthroat (it sounds better than smart and aggressive), blame the winner for winning.

Irony is unappreciated in the software business. When CA bought Chicago-based Pansophic in 1991 for $282 million, it was buying the company that made CA possible. The very first program that CA sold was a piece of software owned by a Swiss company, which had licensed the marketing rights to Pansophic, which, unable to do anything with it, had cleverly given it up. Which is how CA acquired the marketing rights to its first program and its first winner. The rest is (software) history: within a few years CA had absorbed the Swiss company in a reverse acquisition and, sixteen years after it had rescued the original program from Pansophic, acquired Pansophic too. Not enough? When CA acquired ADR, no one seemed to notice that this was the purest metaphor going: the most untraditional software company had swallowed the grandfather of all software outfits, the one generally considered to have been America's first software company, holder of the country's first software patent.

CA's hardheadedness in sales and marketing is paralleled in its pragmatic approach to software development itself. Unlike most companies, CA has been able not only to make decisions quickly—how and why, we'll get into shortly—but also to implement quickly. Its genius at software development is not the genius of inspiration but of putting together the right people to do the right jobs now so that it can all be ready next week, not next year. This is not academic but industrial, not science but engineering. When a new basic principle of thinking machines is discovered, CA will not be the one to do the discovering but will instead have a dozen commercially attractive products or enhancements to existing products up and running on computers as diverse as IBM mainframes and Apple Macintosh desktops, and many capable of working at the same time with different types of software. "Not invented here" is not a problem at CA. Maybe it wasn't invented here, but hell, it works.

17

This approach is often criticized by other developers as a distastefully capitalistic response to external stimuli, as if the goal of a corporation traded on the New York Stock Exchange ought to be what Charles calls "more [expletive] solutions to nonexistent problems." This is a little like Detroit (still) criticizing Japan for producing cars that people actually want. Indeed, CA's approach is so market-oriented that if you close one eye, it may be looked upon as a nontechnology company; the technology is the response, not the impetus. If so, it's clear the CA approach will work if the market is calling for freeze-dried bananas, two-seat sports cars, or underwater glue.

The same recent economic downturn, for example, that had manufacturers in most fields tearing out their hair because clients had stopped spending became a reason for CA last year to create new products that clients could afford. When a software package built around a very useful function found clients who liked it but were unwilling or unable to shake loose $50,000, CA neither discounted the product nor sat around waiting for the economy to improve. Both approaches are passive. Instead, CA developers simply undeveloped the product, removing from the package everything but its very attractive basic functionality so that marketing could offer it for $7,500. That the response was phenomenal is almost incidental to our point. Try to imagine the impact of a U.S. auto company with a hot new turbocharged sports sedan deciding that if the sedan is too expensive why not sell the turbochargers as a pop-in upgrade for older cars? In effect, such an approach creates two markets: one for the turbocharger itself, one for subsequent upgrades. This doesn't merely reengineer the product—it reengineers the entire solution by reengineering the problem.

Of course, reengineering takes time. Not only does the corporate level have to be introduced to the problem, study it, and make the appropriate decision, but from that point the market must be thoroughly researched. Time and money must be spent on surveys. A list of possible approaches must be prepared for submission to the highest levels. Only after this is it decided that the product can be designed. Designs must then be approved. Manufacturing time and space has to be set aside, and usually new personnel hired, because existing personnel are busy doing other things. Then there is manufacturing. Like any other industrial product, software is manufactured, and it is manufactured by being written. But to order up the right product, the specs have to be right, and so does the execution, which must be closely monitored. Meanwhile, the product has to be advertised, promoted. It needs a name. For any new product in the software (or any other) industry, memos must be circulated so that the diverse groups working to hammer things out are all using the same information, from the broadest of policy guidelines to the smallest of details. Then there's packaging, the literature accompanying the product, the literature for point of sale. Of course, the advertising campaign must be coordinated in a timely fashion with the sales force; pricing and commissions have to be set. Just considering the contracts and memos that must be written to cover all of this, it's a wonder anything comes to market at all.

Unless, of course, we're talking about CA. Immediately after the decision to undevelop was made by an individual—not voted on by a group—development began pulling out of the existing software the basic functionality that would allow it to be sold so much more cheaply. (Then the same developers went back to the projects they had interrupted.) Someone in marketing was given responsibility and talked to someone in sales who had been given responsibility. On a run-through someone else noticed that the developers had neglected to change the name of the program. A new name was chosen, as much out of a hat as anything else, so the whole thing went temporarily back to the developers, who interrupted their current project again to switch the names.

Committees? None. Memos? None. Personnel involved: eight. Time expended: two weeks. Not counting point of sale though, because an administrative assistant had to spend an hour or two extra typing up introductory coupons with an expiration date and printing them out on a simple laser printer so the coupons would be ready for the product's debut at a software conference in Atlanta (where the same assistant appeared at a special table to distribute them). The product was so attractive at the price that salespeople around the country became involved in a brisk side business in acquiring properly dated coupons for their clients.

To say that another software company would take years, not days, to develop and launch such a product is only to begin to understand how different CA is from its competitors—and by extension, from companies in many other businesses. Yet people at CA themselves are often unaware of it, especially those who have have never worked at another company. As a corporation, CA may not in fact have really come to terms with its own uniqueness until mid-1987. Though it had already acquired fourteen companies, none of them had been the size of Dallas-based Uccel, then the world's second-largest software company and CA's principal rival, a company so different from CA that the takeover was to become an $800 million learning experience.

The clash of cultures was so extreme that during negotiations, when Uccel's management group, its attorneys, economists, and financial advisers waited in a conference room for the arrival of the parallel CA team, only Charles and his brother Anthony W. Wang, president of CA, showed up. Every eye in the room kept watching the door in anticipation of what to Uccel sensibilities should have been a dozen more suits. It was to be a long wait.

The confrontation calls to mind another tale chasing around Texas at the same time: After many nights of serious rioting in a Rio Grande border town, the town council called in the Texas Rangers to send down a force to subdue the hundreds of armed drunks in the streets. Gathered at the station to meet the train, the town fathers were shocked to see only one Ranger step down onto the platform.

The mayor rushed up to protest: "We got us a serious situation here—we expected more than one man."

The Ranger, adjusting his Stetson, replied, "Why, you don't have but one riot, do you?"

Uccel's riot was singular, but it was large. With its leadership stratified into layers upon layers, Uccel spent lavishly on salaries and perks for the least productive managers. Development followed the industry standard by producing solutions in an ivory tower before dropping them in the lap of marketing, which was expected to find a problem the solutions could solve. Having acquired five companies the same year it was itself on the block, Uccel was attempting to run these as totally autonomous units, each with the same administrative superstructure that had gotten it taken over in the first place. And though Uccel had just

21

gone through two layoffs, it was building a huge headquarters tower in Dallas with a four-thousand-square-foot office for the chairman, whose rule epitomized that style of management perhaps best described as "death by M.B.A."

Of course, Uccel's employees, who expected brutal treatment from their own management, expected worse from CA, including wholesale firings. But there was more to it than fear. There was resentment.

CA was clearly the outsider in the software industry. Its management had no patina of Ivy League education and connections; though Tony had been a scholarship student at Yale, Charles and his development wizard, Russell M. Artzt, were graduates of Queens College, a no-tuition New York City school with all the ivy you might expect to find at an airport. CA's sales force was even more uncouth. A good many did not buy their clothes at Brooks Brothers. They talked with peculiar accents, the most comfortingly familiar of which was New York–ese. The racial mixture was perhaps too vivid. Besides, CA was seen to have a secretive and therefore sneaky nature.

In fact, a lot of the close-to-the-vest stuff at CA was real, an outgrowth of Charles' suspicion that his company's quick decision making, lack of bureaucracy, and maverick management style would be seen by Wall Street as shoot-from-the-hip one-man rule. With no CA public relations department to counteract rumor and innuendo, the software industry's captive press had every reason to distrust CA, as did the Wall Street analysts who read that press and the finance writers who lunched with the analysts. Never was the imminent failure of so successful a firm so often and so confidently announced.

On the other hand, all this fear and trembling made sense: its competitors saw CA as a ruthless opponent (true) that always kept a pocketful of cash (also true) in order to be able to buy those competitors (very true) that were not as well run (exponentially true).

The irony in all this was lost not only on the industry but on CA itself, which looked upon the companies it acquired with a kind of grudging respect for their inefficient pyramidal structures and wasteful executive suites, while at the same time knowing these were the reasons the same companies were failures and ripe for CA's takeover. It was quite as if Judy Garland and Mickey Rooney had just said "Come on, gang, let's put on a show!" but at the same time remained in awe of the overstaged, overpaid, and talentless hoofers and singers they would replace. When it came down to it, however, there was no question: when CA acquired a company, the company lost a lot of weight.

Which is why Charles was so happy to have found Sanjay Kumar in the rat's nest of underemployed yes-men and quitters on the executive level at Uccel. Charles must have felt he had found someone very much like himself.

Sanjay was clearly someone he could trust to bring order to Uccel's internal chaos. Charles himself, meanwhile, had to deal with the problem of how Uccel—a rigidly pyramided corporation that functioned, like the Kremlin, from the top down—could most smoothly be melded into a Computer Associates, whose modus operandi resembled, depending on the observer, an overconfident band of tiring guerrilla warriors (this from Wall Street analysts who consistently disliked what they could not understand), the Mafia (present and future objects of takeover have the affection for CA a lame shrew has for an agile twelve-pound tomcat), or a basketball team run by a tough player-manager (more or less the view from inside the company).

A cynic might have said Charles picked Sanjay as the man to trust at Uccel out of incipient Asian solidarity, which would be wrong. But altered a bit, the reflection makes sense: he may have been drawn to Sanjay, now CA senior vice president for planning, because both had been in the same boat, and it wasn't the *Mayflower*.

Within a year after arriving from Sri Lanka as a teenager and settling with his family in a small apartment in Greenville, South Carolina, Sanjay bumped into his first computer. Sanjay: "In high school a friend's father owned a computer, Apple I back then, and didn't know what to do with it. He had a distribution outfit. One day I borrowed the book that came with the computer. To do anything, you had to code everything in machine language, very difficult. I didn't know anything about computers, but I read the book and said, *Oh, this is a neat toy*, and I got the computer to do what my friend's father needed. He paid me five hundred dollars. I thought five hundred dollars was a lot of money. Before long a couple of my friend's father's friends looked at it and said, 'Gee, this is pretty slick.' They said, 'You can do the same for me.' So I went back to the original guy and said, 'You don't have to pay up—just give me the program I offered you, and I'll help you update it.' Now I owned a piece of software. So I changed a few lines here, put a new title on the screen, and set myself up a little software business." **Sanjay had discovered, like Charles and like millions of other immigrants and their children, that he had talent—and that it could be valued in cash.** Sanjay:

24

"So one day I went to college, I was going to be a doctor, premed major. Hated school with a passion. To this day I do not like the education system in this country—such a waste; they let the mind rot. I was doing things in high school here that I was doing in seventh grade in Sri Lanka. College was such a joke. I worked two jobs when I was in college. Worked at school, worked at two jobs outside. It was great. Fixed all the college computers so that all my classes would wind up in the morning so I'd have the rest of the day to work. I had a choice to make, whether I was going into medicine or something else. Everybody told me the money was in medicine. I said, 'Look, I'm making too much money the way it is and having too much fun. Forget medicine.' So from there I had a couple of jobs and worked for a company in South Carolina, developed system software there, which they turned around and gave to a company named Uccel. Uccel started courting me, and eventually they said, 'Ah, come work for us.' So after the fourth time they asked me in two years to come work for them, I said to myself, *They must really be in trouble. I'm not going anywhere they're flying high—why bother, you're just one guy in a camp that's going 'Rah-rah-rah,' right? You want to go somewhere where there are problems so you can turn it around, where you can matter.* And Uccel was really in trouble. Culture was very different from what I later found at CA. Layers of management. The chairman would walk in with a bodyguard, bald-headed guy name of Pierre." **At a certain stage, though, selling your brainpower clashes head-on with the type of organization that buys it.** Sanjay: "The guy that ran Uccel was an M.B.A. type. If he got bored at meetings, he'd tell you to shut up and walk out. He had this stretch limo that would pull up to the side of the building. Pierre would get out, open the door for the chairman, and then run through the building and get in the elevator. The chairman was not far behind, so no one got in. If you saw Pierre in the elevator, you didn't get in. It went straight to the tenth floor. The tenth floor had a card access, you couldn't get in there unless you were one of the select executives in the company. The chairman's mission in life was to turn around and sell the company. That's what he wanted to do. And I think everyone knew that and no one liked him for it. Now, of course, I think that's a very strange company, but then I kind of saw it as normal. A lot of in-fighting. Wasn't a team." **Because the impetus that drives the management of a normal company is not the creation of wealth.** Sanjay: "A few months after I moved to Dallas to work for Uccel, the merger happened. I'll never forget that day ever. I worked for a guy named Mike, who had started a month before I moved to Dallas to run the systems software division. His predecessor recruited me. After I agreed to come to Dallas, I knew he was leaving. That's why I came there, and I also knew they were going to bring in a guy to replace Mike, who was not technical. You can't have an M.B.A. run something like this. You need somebody who's technical. He was lost, and I knew he would need a right-hand man to run it. And so when you have two people in front of you and you're the new guy on the block, who do you side with, another new guy or the nine guys who thought they should have had your job? I was the tenth guy." **It is the preservation of the hierarchy.** Sanjay: "He looked to me to run the organization day to day, which is very good. I liked that. The day the thing happened, I got a call from him. We had three buildings in Dallas. He was in the headquarters building, and he said, 'I got to give you some news,' and I said, 'We're being merged with another company.' (Officially it was a merger.) Ten minutes before that call I had a phone call from New York from a friend who said, 'Do you know this is happening?' So I knew. I said to Mike, 'Yeah, I know—it's probably a good thing." **So the threat to business as usual must be countered.** Sanjay: "He was shocked: 'Like, CA, you know who they are?' And I said, 'Yeah, they're not too bad.' 'No,' he said. 'This is terrible.' " **And the defense is often emotional.** Sanjay: "I said, 'Mike, you're starting off on the wrong foot. You think it's terrible, everyone will think it's terrible.' And from that day on, until the merger was completed, there was not one good word said about CA in that place, not one." **The character of these aggressive new players must be attacked.** Sanjay: "The word was: CA, it's cheap, cutthroat, nonprofessional, can't be trusted. Cheap. They didn't have an ivory tower development program like Uccel, they weren't building a new building, they didn't pay well. Cheap in every sense of the word. Frugal beyond belief. Run by a couple of guys who do not delegate any decision-making authority. That's the image that was going on. And that they'll cut fifty percent of the staff. Which was bad enough just after the announcement on June 1, but the transaction did not consummate until late August while we waited for the Justice Department to finish looking at it. While this dragged on, the company was paralyzed, existing management was totally ineffective—they all knew they were going to be gone. People didn't do anything because existing management kept feeding them lines of garbage that life was not going to be good anymore. Everybody was looking for a job, everybody." **Whether through demonization or willful ignorance, the policy is denial. To see things otherwise would be to admit that something is wrong with the way business was being done up to now.** Sanjay: "So I spent the first three days educating people about CA. No one knew anything about CA. Uccel was living in its own little world—

they didn't know anything about anybody. CA was the competition. But they didn't know. Most technicians didn't even know. That to me was strange. Maybe I know more than the average person about the business as a whole, but I thought they should have known more than what they did about their own business. In a sense they didn't have to know, because Uccel was run from the top down. Nobody had to know anything. But now jobs were on the line, so every manager in the place would call me up and ask me about CA. I kept up on the industry—still do. The executives wanted my files on CA. I had copies of annual reports. And they wanted copies, were coming to me in droves, and they wanted to see what Charles and Tony looked like in the damn picture in the annual report. I was called three or four times by different groups to educate them on CA products so the executives would look intelligent when Charles and Tony spoke to them. Some were trying to save their hide because they knew that Charles and Tony like hands-on people. There had been a lot of sleeping going on, but they woke up. Then came the big meeting. Word came out that Charles was going to come speak at five o'clock one day, so we all piled into an auditorium. To the CA people there, it was just a simple meeting, but they didn't realize what had happened at Uccel six months before. Uccel had had two big layoffs, handled terribly. One of the layoffs was so bad and so confusing people didn't know what they were doing—so bad the support telephones didn't get answered for a day—and people thought then that Uccel had the best support in the business. They would scream that CA support was bad and Uccel was the best. For a day or more those telephones did not get answered because people had been invited to the same—the very same—auditorium to see new org charts flashed on the screen. If you were there, you were there, and if you weren't, you didn't have a job. So for a lot of people it was kind of a déjà vu feeling, not a good feeling to be back in the same auditorium. So Charles spoke, did a joke. Said, 'Next time I come by, I hope all of you will wave, very vigorously, but with all five fingers.' " **Even admitting the possibility is tantamount to an admission that everything that had been done up to now is wrong.** Sanjay: "He was very up front. It shocked most people. Someone asked him if there were going to be cuts, and he said, 'Yes.' What area? 'Well, I don't really need two finance departments, two personnel departments. Technical, we'll have to look. Sales, we'll have to look. But I'll let people know day one.' And to date he has never waivered in that in an acquisition, which I think is one of our strengths. It is something we get black eyes over because on one day we cut so many people, while if someone else were doing it, they wouldn't cut anyone immediately, but every day for a year you didn't know if you had a job because they kept cutting and cutting and cutting. That isn't the CA way. Charles was totally up-front. On D-Day of the Uccel deal, I had to let thirty people go, thirty-some-odd people." **The villain can't be us—it must be them.** Sanjay: "So after the meeting, the next day Charles and Russ and some others stayed, and each of the product-group managers gave a presentation, and we went through all our stuff, took furious notes." **Yet there are always people who are flexible enough to understand there might be another way.** Sanjay: "We were introduced to the CA note-books that day, all the CA guys, Charles, Tony, Russ, and the others whipped out these school-kid notebooks to take notes in, and the Uccel guys—they couldn't make a phone call without a secretary—just looked at them. Well, at dinner that night we all got along so well. It was a great dinner, and I had spoken to Charles earlier that day and I knew it would all be okay. These are okay guys. Matter of hours, I had made up my mind—these guys are all right." **Sanjay saw it immediately.** Sanjay: "Then came D-Day. I knew when D-Day was gonna be, I didn't know how many other people did. Charles and Tony and everybody came down. The night before, the CA people met with a bunch of Uccel managers who would be the people doing the terminations the next morning. That night after the group broke up, Charles, Russ, and I met and got everything worked out on my organization, and it was a vote of confidence because they agreed with what I thought it should look like. Next morning we met, and Charles whipped out his famous 'term' sheets. You got these people you term. How he came up with these lists is each of the Uccel managers had to rank their people. Essentially Charles went through and said, 'Development—this group has thirty people, it should have twenty, take out the bottom ten. Administration, I need the top two in accounts payable, I don't need the other eight.' The day came, and you hand out the sheets by terminator, who are the people who terminate. And we set up a little headquarters in the boardroom at Uccel, gorgeous room full of gadgets and gizmos and a beautiful table. Charles sat there with his PC and every hour we would call and give him a checkpoint, saying, 'Look, the following people know they are gone.' My original list was twenty-four, but it ended up being thirty-six, because some of the managers didn't know some of their own people. That's the kind of company Uccel was. A very difficult day. I'm telling people they don't have a career: 'I'm sorry to do it, but you got to know today. I don't believe in waiting six months and then telling you that I don't need you anymore.' By eleven A.M. it was done. Twelve o'clock there was a meeting at the Ramada

Hotel down by Uccel headquarters for all the people who were staying. Charles went over the new organization, outlined it to everybody, and told them this is the way it is going to be and we were part of CA. The hardest part was getting them to understand that there would not be another layoff. They could not buy that. They would not buy it. They just kept saying, 'No, no, no, we are going to have another layoff.' Well, there was not another cut, and we didn't plan one. Even in the back of our minds, we don't have a secret little plan that if this doesn't work out, we'll cut another twenty percent. If there is going to be a cut there is going to be a cut once and once alone. The hardest part was getting them to see that."

The training ground of corporate employees is the corporation. Sanjay: "We had months of bitching. CA does it this way, we used to do it that way. One day I called a meeting of all the people I had and said, 'Look, it's time to commit or get off the pot. You're not going to stay on the fence anymore. I have given in to all the requests you guys have. I've bent over backward. I've gotten Charles to change a few policies, which he had never changed before for CA.' For example, at one time CA handed out telephone credit cards for employees. For people who want to call at night, they could call customers using the credit card. Convenient, right? Well, somebody used it to call a couple of foreign countries, talked to his in-laws for ten hours, built up a few thousand dollars. So Charles said, 'Screw this, no more credit cards.' That was an inconvenience. To have the employee charge it on his own bill, sort out the bill at the end of the month, fill it in? It's costing us more money to write these stupid checks than we were paying out. An inconvenience, and in my opinion we weren't managing the problem. The problem was the employee who was abusing the card. Kick the SOB out, fire him, and sue him. Don't penalize everybody else. Everybody else said, 'No, forget about it, because Charles decided no.' So I went to Charles. I sat down and said, 'This doesn't make sense. Give me as a manager the responsibility to manage the problem. If I fail and I have a bunch of guys that are calling Australia for pizza, let me can them. If I let it go on for a couple of months and I know about it, kick me out the door. Give me the responsibility, the accountability, and give me the authority that goes with it.' He said, 'OK.' " **What they are used to is what they come to expect.** Sanjay: "Hey, he said OK. So I had some confidence and was able to go to my guys and say, 'Do it or get off the pot.' About five people left right after, but the others were OK. After that things began to run smoothly. Much more smoothly. We started doing things, started working as a team, got technical people from here to come down there. We still had some problems with ex-sales-people who went with competitors, but that smoothed out over time. And then I picked up a couple other products, and that was a true sign that we were being successful in Dallas. Charles gave us some of the CA products to run. I picked up the Phoenix Developmental Center, which had been Capex, the first company CA bought, in 1982. I got the L.A. center and a couple of others on the East Coast. And another true test was when I closed Phoenix. I couldn't get any productive work out of them. So I shut the place down. And that was good. It sent two messages. It sent a message to those managers that joined CA, saying, 'Yeah, you guys can take responsibility, take on accountability, he'll give you the room. If you do well, he is going to pat you on the back and reward you, and if you mess up, he is going to blame you for it—not someone else, you.' It also sent quite a few people the message to get off the dime. 'Do some work or CA is going to close you down. CA is not going to be held hostage.' And we were being held hostage by the group in Phoenix for a long time. I finally faced up to that problem, and shortly thereafter I closed the development center in L.A. too. We made some hard choices. But every time we fire people, we are not firing people, we're replacing them with better people. Not necessarily more-talented people, but more-willing people, people who bring a good attitude. The people at Uccel were used to the kind of corporate life they had at Uccel—nobody had ever told them, 'Hey, work like hell and do great things and we'll make you rich and you'll be happy to go to work in the morning.' You'd think it was the simplest thing in the world, but in every takeover we've had—I mean companies in deep trouble, looking for help—the same people, most of them, can't realize that there's a very simple way to do things."

So clearly things must change. Sanjay: "So there it is, same basic ideas, same products, same people sometimes—only one works and one doesn't. One succeeds and one doesn't. One gets taken over and one does the taking over." **Especially now.** Sanjay: "What always amazes me is people think you have to be a computer programming genius to figure that out. But it couldn't be more simple. One way may have worked in the past. But it doesn't now." **On the eve of a new century.**

II. Products

When Charles Wang began Computer Associates in 1976, he had never managed anything but a failure. That failure was a computer software consultancy he had begun with Russell Artzt, a college friend who is now CA's chief of development. Very quickly Charles discovered that what he was selling was his and Russ's own time, for which he could charge higher and higher fees but of which the supply was by nature limited. Such a company could grow, but only by adding additional consultants. This means that the same limitations on profitability would merely be multiplied. Or as the irate diner complained to the waiter, "The food is terrible—and the portions are so small." Charles determined to find a product. Charles: "The first company I had was a company I started about three years after college. With Russ. It was a consulting type company. Closed it finally. We said, 'This is the wrong business. We need products.' So we went off and started to build products. Started to get rights to products and build products because we learned. Consulting? Forget it. What we were doing is just a high-class lawyer or whore, whichever one is lower and I'm not sure. I used to tell my brother, Tony, when he was a lawyer, 'You're just a high-priced hooker, that's all. You sell your time. I'm going to build capital. I'm going to build products that I can just stamp them out.' You've got to have a product. That's when I decided, I'm going to build products."

The first of those products turned out to be a sorting program for IBM mainframes, and the choosing and acquisition of it would

34

make a nice chapter in any book about starting a business. Charles: "At first, the products we distributed, we got a percentage of every sale, so it ends up basically salaries, telephone bills—you didn't have to travel. When we started up, I sold only by phone. The computer time we bartered because we were doing support for American Can Company, and the office space we bartered. Everything was sold on trials, trials, that's all. I said, 'Try it, you'll like it, try it, you'll like it, try it, you'll like it.' Glorious time—so much business, you wouldn't believe. Crazy. Sure, other people were trying to do the same thing. They picked the wrong products probably. We picked the right product. It's a product that everybody needs. It's a product everybody knows. It's a product that has its payoff day one. So when you sort through all of them, you end up with a utility product that is totally compatible to what they're using, so there's no training. Sorting was the best one, right on the money. Bang. That was the criteria: it saves your machine resources. Bingo. So from the moment we started, we were driven by the needs of the market, absolutely, and to make it so painless, so easy, I'd send it to you on trial, you put it up—you don't change one program, nothing—you just put it up, and it runs faster. You can't beat that. It's like giving somebody a light bulb that lasts ten times as long for a lower price. Put in a couple and you know. Immediately, you know. Meanwhile, the European company we got it from was selling the same product over there and not doing well. Why? Because we did promotions. Campaigns. I built a little test data generator that Russ and I worked on together. Then we gave it away if you tried the sort product. We tried everything. In Europe they were still thinking they were consultants because that was the basis of their company. They were still thinking they were a consulting company. So when they went out into the market they would actually send *people*. I would never visit anybody. What am I visiting you for? I'll give you a lower price on the product even, just so long as I don't have to visit you. Why am I visiting you? To install it? No, you don't need that. To talk to you about it? We're talking, why am I visiting? One guy says, 'Because you can pick up the check while you're here.' I said, 'You I'm visiting—when do you want me there?' That's how we started." Obviously the choice was right, but now that Charles had discovered a potential market, he had to get new products. Unlike adding new consultants, additional products would generate profits geometrically rather than arithmetically.

Essentially there are two ways to add products: acquire the right to sell them or create new ones. Charles pursued both courses, but each had its limitation.

Products already developed were often not quite suited for the market; those created in-house had a way of simply re-creating software that had already been created elsewhere. Charles synthesized the two: software produced outside was enhanced so as to work together with software already being sold or on its way to the market; software produced in-house was increasingly targeted toward creating the bridges that would allow diverse software to work together or toward filling product needs—say, three software programs needed two other entirely new programs to create a comprehensive new product line. Charles: "In a lot of companies, *high-tech* usually means 'let's make a product and see later if it sells.' That's stupid-tech. We're high-tech beyond the word. Yes, we imitate. We don't develop what I call elegant solutions in search of problems. We go and focus on what our client requirements are, where we see the market as it is or we're laying down the foundations for the future market."

III. People

Early on, this approach, wonderfully successful, was no different from any other entrepreneurial tack. But Charles went further: if the products themselves were either commonly acquirable or easily buildable, what was to distinguish CA from other software companies that were not doing as well? Luck? Even were this true, the circumstances for continued good fortune could not be re-created at will. Timing? Part of that was still luck, but part doubtlessly was human initiative. What part, then, did people play? Whatever part it was, it was clearly the only part that could be cultivated.

Charles: "It all comes down to a couple of very simple things, which are: One, we've got to get people. People who work for you. Work for you. But they've got to have reasons. They want to have a sense of career and that what they say has some impact. They've got to know their contribution has some meaning. You don't want to work for something where you just punch in, be there for so many hours. That's mindless, and people will resent that, and that's when you polarize groups. So you get them involved in decisions. Ask them. Make mistakes, but correct them, and make sure the people are always heard. The second piece of it is they want to have fun doing it. You've got to have a relaxed kind of driven. Driven but relaxed."

It's doubtful that one day Charles Wang slapped his forehead and shouted "Aha!" CA was growing so fast that he simply had

37

to decide either to control it or to find people to help it grow even faster. CA had become something of a rapids. Either the water source could be dammed and the rapids turned into a slow-moving and predictable river, or it could be allowed to run free and follow the shape of the market by creating new channels, which would of necessity be the fastest flowing and the most treacherous.

Charles pushed the nose of the company into the current. But to run in those channels without being swept away would require paddling faster than the current. Finding people he trusted to do this became the company's number one priority. Charles: "The important thing is this can-do attitude. It's a damn-the-torpedoes, full-speed-ahead, ready-aim-fire approach that says the hell with anything else, and it's that kind of take-charge, we-can-do-it, nothing-can-defeat-us people who move ahead and it doesn't matter where. In other companies, people with that kind of attitude don't move ahead, they keep hitting this wall, and they pile up or leave. They leave—or get acquired, the whole company. Here that's what gets people ahead. What kind of person succeeds at CA? I say self-moti-vated people. Hungry people, people who have been through a little pain in life. First-generation immigrants—they know, they've seen their parents struggle, people who arrived in this country with three suitcases, two suitcases. They've seen struggle, they've seen people go to school at night. They know. Something about Queens, Brooklyn people—they are so down-to-earth. You know the people. They come out of city schools, and there is something about them, there is a hustle in them, a thing that says, 'I can do it, and if I can't, I'll find a way—it's not a big deal.' That's the kind of people who succeed. The ones who don't succeed are the ones that come from big companies up to here with cover-your-ass memos: 'Everything has to be researched a hundred times before we move.' We go more by gut."

Software as an industry at this time was undergoing unprece-dented growth, mostly fueled by massive infusions of venture capital that kept many companies going, most of them hopeless, all on the gamble there would be a spectacular payoff down the road. Good managers were hard to find, not least because stan-dards for managers in the software industry were perversely different than in any other field. The measure of a manager in software was not success but its promise. The greater the prom-ise, the greater the manager. Marvelously innovative but totally unmotivated by profit and loss, these technician-managers ei-ther loved the rapids so much they drowned in them or spent years in software eddies that had little commercial application. Charles: "We're a mostly sales- and marketing-driven com-pany. We put it together with marketing more than other companies, so the development people can develop what the marketing people want, what the salespeople say is required by their clients. It's straightforward." Equally unsuitable were professional managers armed with solid M.B.A.'s from the best schools. These were not adventurers. Like nineteenth-century sea captains, they had been trained to competently guide the corporate ship from port to predictable port. They might know enough to survive the odd storm, but such professional adminis-trators of the status quo were hardly the stuff for rapids. Charles: "This bureaucracy bull—cut that away. The people who want that are not the kind of people we want. One of the greatest things is, we don't like M.B.A.'s. They've learned all the wrong things. Teaching you to climb the corporate ladder. I want self-starters, I don't want ass-kissers. Sure they know how to do reports, memos, business plans, and all that. But I don't need that. I need doers."

Like most of us in a crisis, Charles turned to those he felt he could trust. Charles: "I used to get Tony's shirts." **Starting with his brother.**

IV. Trust

In recruiting Tony Wang, a corporate lawyer from a Wall Street firm, CA got a man who not only knew nothing about software but has since spent a decade not learning much more. Not only does Charles' elder brother still not use a computer, he had never managed anything. Now Tony was president of a company doing hundreds of millions of dollars a year and growing fast. Mistake? What Tony brought to CA was neither technical ability nor the kind of management skills learned from years of climbing the corporate ladder by smoothly murmuring "Yes" at each rung. Tony brought a cool, nearly serene intelligence that perfectly balanced Charles' visionary passion. When a decision was being made, Tony broke it down into consequences. And he could say anything to Charles, because each shared the other's indelible trust. Tony: "There are lots of people who can do what I do. Years ago I was at a deposition on a law suit, and one of the questions was what was my title and what do I do? I said I don't know." Such constructive nepotism was nothing new at CA. Judy Cedeno, Charles' administrative assistant, has brought in as many as nine close family members, including her sister, Betty Santiago, who assists Tony. Half of CA seems to have a relative or childhood friend on the payroll. But Tony's arrival was the most glaring. Had he come on board after CA went public, analysts at the brokerage houses would have recommended an immediate sell. Chairmen of firms listed on the New York Stock Exchange are not supposed to recruit on the basis of absolute trust.

41

Then, on the same basis, Tony recruited Arnie Mazur, a buddy from the same white-shoe law firm. At least Arnie signed on as a lawyer, so his lack of management or computer experience would be immaterial. Less outrageous? Not really. Within months he was running marketing. Next he turned up in London to reinvigorate and expand CA's international operations. Then he took over sales. And he too still doesn't know how to use a computer.

He did, however, bring in Michael J. Picker, an accountant. After a stint doing internal audit, Mike was sent to head up the company's ailing marketing services group, responsible for the design, printing, binding, warehousing, and distribution of every piece of paper with a CA logo on it, including endless updates of highly technical documentation that must find their way on time to thousands of CA employees and customers. Mike: "I started to work with Charles on projects and side projects, and finally he said, basically, 'You have a little common sense, I think you work well with people, so why don't you go to this marketing services group.' I said I knew nothing about marketing, I didn't go to any school for marketing. He said, 'The only way you can study marketing the right way is one on one. Don't worry. You have common sense.' " Mike Picker, now a senior vice president, is Arnie Mazur's nephew.

Charles had set in motion a form of recruitment that would have buried other companies. It is, in fact, the principal reason most family firms fail. But it is also the principal reason they succeed. Good family relationships and friendships share with good businesses three unbuyable qualities: those involved know each other well, will go to great lengths to put out for one another, and can be trusted. This does not mean everyone's cousin gets a job, nor does it mean that Charles is willing to tolerate less than exemplary achievement simply because of a personal relationship, family or otherwise. Charles: "Even if it's someone you like personally, OK, you'll probably give him more room, but ultimately you've got to be fair, you've got to be evenhanded about it. You're not going to be evenhanded every day. Just like you don't get up in the morning and say you love CA every day. It doesn't happen that way, either. You've got to average it out over a long period of time. But you've got to have the integrity of being honest, being brutally honest if you have to be, just telling people where it's at, exactly where they stand, no matter who they are or how they came to CA." But it does mean that an essential part of the recruitment process can be leapfrogged: the new person may not work out—and if that's the case, the person can be let go, or his or her authority can be restricted—but the person is a known quantity from day one. By extension, the process allows Charles to tap the close friends and family of CA personnel at every level and at every remove from the chairman's office. If CA can trust someone to run a $100 million section of the company, it can trust the same person not to bring in a stiff. Tony: "There's a comfort level in working with people you know and trust. I've known Arnie since 1968. In our professional lives we've grown up together. With someone like that, I never have to worry about a hidden agenda. But there are also many situations of people close to us who for whatever reason didn't work out. When that happens, we don't carry the family." By monitoring performance and remaining clear-eyed about judging it, CA had developed a chain of nepotism that is not nepotism at all. Because it works.

But not well enough. Industrial-strength friends and relations are always in short supply. And CA has grown so fast that it has had, on average, to find larger headquarters buildings every three years. No one has that many relatives. All the while new people were signing on, both individually and in clumps, as CA began to acquire other companies. In sixteen years it has absorbed forty-two firms.

V. Growth

Most American high-tech acquisitions vacuum up people with experience in fields the acquirer needs. CA, however, has never targeted talent. Charles looks instead for products to meld into CA's software line, access to new markets, a customer base. Charles: "You look at the financials, you look at the product, you look at the sales. Then you ask, 'How's it all going to fit in to where we're going? How does this part make it all greater than just adding the pieces together? How do we leverage off what they've got or what we've got?' If they have a product that I can sell through my sales force, God bless, that's great, then I have leverage beyond what they have standing alone. If they need one piece for their product to make it successful and I happen to have that piece—graphics, say—then that's another leverage. If we put this together with what we have, it's a whole new product, going to knock the socks off the industry. But that's just short-term. The strategic stuff has nothing to do with today. There are certain things we have to be in four, five years down the road. We better have the foundation built for those." **Charles' clear goal from the outset was to build the world's best independent software company, and he had found the way.** Nancy Li, senior vice president, research and development: "There's the perception out there that because we've acquired so many companies, our products are like a K mart—that we bought this one from here and that one from there, and then we package them and sell them. But within each area we've done a lot of architecting, taking what's good in the new products and merging it in with the overall vision to create this layer and allowing us to be independent of any of the hardware platforms. That's a lot of investment that people don't realize CA has done and which has allowed us to keep coming out with new products—and absorb companies, because without having laid this down, things would really go crazy. We would end up just being a distributor. But that's no value to the client because all you would have is these disparate products that don't talk to each other and don't add value to each other. And it would make our efforts so much greater. We'd keep re-creating the same thing. Instead of taking a piece of code, a piece of technology that's already been developed, we'd have to redo it. This way it's modular, it's shared."

While CA was not looking specifically for personnel when it made an acquisition, they joined as part of the deal. But trying to incorporate them into CA —CA-izing them—was to make it woefully apparent how distinctive a culture Charles Wang had created. Nancy: "In development you've got to know their strengths and their weaknesses, where to put them, how to get them motivated. But when you have two big acquisitions one after the other, ADR followed by Cullinet, in both companies people got very demoralized, even the survivors. They don't see the light anymore. So what you've got is a segment of development that's still the way they always were, and then you've got another segment that works so differently. The difference is extreme. CA developers, they kind of own things. Anything they see that they can do, they follow up. They follow through. But you've got companies like ADR and Cullinet that built such a gigantic bureaucracy to a point where people just sit there and wait to be told what to do. They have this mind-set that any task is just impossible, insurmountable. And what happens when you have this discrepancy? We have these techno meetings where we exchange information—we don't want people to re-create the wheel. If you're going to create something, create something new—not something that's already been done and just do it a little differently, because that's not making anything new. But that's the mind-set. And you can't go out and fire the whole company. Maybe you should, though that wouldn't be fair because you don't know if there are some very good developers who have never been managed and you don't know who's good and who's bad. So for a whole period of time you're just evaluating your new people. However, that's affecting the group here because you're so busy with the new group you're leaving so many good people unmanaged. With the geographical situation, so much distance between offices, you have to pick somebody from this other group, the acquired group, to lead, and he just doesn't measure up. It's just so apparent. He's lethargic. No matter what you talk about, they can only complain about what's wrong. They don't do solutions. You know what I'm saying? You can say, 'This is screwed up,' and then you offer how you're going to fix it. But everything you suggest is not right. That was the thing. That was the hardest part, how not to lower standards because you've got different groups. How do you weed out within this group the stars or the people that have the potential? Sometimes I think we could have gotten so much more stuff done if I didn't have to do this. Both Russ and I went to Charles and said, 'Why the heck did you acquire these companies?' Not to say that the other group doesn't need to be managed because it can be very dynamic and so forth, but I spent a good year on this acquisition, and every day some new issue comes up. What do you do if you've got people in support, which is easy to measure—development is hard to measure, but support is easy: it's the number of problems you solve, the number of calls you take—so what do you do when you've got such discrepancies? You've got one group that takes two or three calls per day per person, and the other group, the group here on Long Island, taking twenty. At some point you have to deal with these things. We've always managed by knowing the people, working with them. Some of these new groups, you can't trust the manager, can't trust what he's telling you, and you can't physically be there to see what's going on, so you have to resort to something statistical, factual. At first we weren't used to doing that, so it's painful. Here we had one group on Long Island that was dealing with twenty calls and the other group was taking two or three calls—that's the kind of discrepancy—and they were still hitting on me for more people. And then after a while you're saying, *Should I just close down this whole impossible place?* But you can't, because that's only statistical, on the average, because I'm sure there are people there taking twenty or thirty calls a day and some people doing nothing, which is not fair to the good people."

After a while, acquisitions took a predictable form: the new company's bloated upper management was blown away, its middle management was combed for potential CA types, and these were told to rank the three, five, or hundred best of their own people and dismiss the rest. Ancillary functions, like finance, were absorbed by CA headquarters. This left the crème de la crème of the acquired company, welcomed without reservation into CA. Yet of those who took up CA's offer, few would make the grade. The most successful were often those who had been frustrated by the acquired company's corporate restraints; they flowered at CA. But the dropout rate of acquired employees—

half disappear by the end of their first year—continues to affect the single statistic that Charles is least anxious to divulge, turnover of personnel. He thinks it will lead to criticism of the company, as though the number of college athletes who never make it as professionals is in some sense an indictment of pro sports. CA's general turnover rate is at least 30 percent, from 20 percent in development to 75 percent in sales. This ruthless pruning is a result of the principal aspect of CA that sets it apart from all other American companies.

VI. Change

CA endlessly reinvents itself. In the early days Charles would reorganize the company from scratch as often as four times a year. Charles: "We shake them all up a little bit, which is fine. This place gets boring. Doing the same thing, you get bored. Yeah, because I get bored easily. Listen, I tell it to you exactly the way it is. We get b-o-o-o-red." Nowadays, "reorg" has been more or less institutionalized as a once-a-year restructuring—though no one at CA, least of all Charles himself, is willing to guarantee it won't happen, if necessary, more often. Charles: "You can say we broke the mold, but we never look at the mold. See, that's the nice thing about us. We didn't have the mold. It doesn't matter exactly what the structure is. See, focusing on how we are structured—that has nothing to do with it because we're changing the structure all the time. The quality of the people isn't dependent on the structure. Good people, lousy structure—you still do okay. We don't have a perfect structure. We can't, because we'll always have to change it. Marketing is still in a state of flux. Still not sure. We're probably going to change it again. If you have great structure but lousy people, you're still not going to get it done."

In essence, what CA does could be called corporate recycling, were it not for the unpleasant fact that recycling commodities normally devalues them: high-grade paper is turned into low-grade paper, which on the next recycling is turned into card-

50

board. Take a car whose original market value was twenty thousand dollars and whose current worth is six hundred, and recycle it: you've got forty bucks worth of scrap. But take a collection of human beings and shift them into new jobs with bigger responsibilities so that the corporate organization becomes more creative and efficient, and you have added value.

Not only do people who have been quickly moved into positions of authority grow as individuals, but the company becomes much better at what it must do, which is produce, market, and sell its products. In the driest economic terms, it is getting more out of its assets. In a company whose single significant asset is people, there is no other way. And in a twenty-first century in which every asset that is not people—machines, real estate, money, credit—is merely a commodity, the same principle will apply across the board and in spades.

VII. Stars

CA's remarkable growth from zero to approaching $2 billion in sales in sixteen years is not the result of luck, timing, or the tooth fairy. It is the result of a management ethic which sees people as CA's only true assets.

These assets may resist quantification on a standard balance sheet, but one indication is salary. CA's average annual salary of $48,000 is at least a third higher than that of highly stratified companies like IBM. Unlike IBM, CA does not bother with a salary schedule—you get what you're worth. A rookie programmer starting at $30,000 may see his salary double in a year. And CA is almost certainly the only company in the world willing to pay an engineer not yet out of his twenties a salary, before bonuses, of close to $200,000.

If this sounds like professional sports, the analogy is apt. The engineer's value to CA is as high as that of a star quarterback to a pro football team, and both in pro ball and at CA, stars are sought out, developed, and compensated accordingly. Arnie: "Stars, we're always looking for stars. 'Where are the stars?' We're always asking this question, and always looking." Considering that a pro quarterback's value diminishes rapidly after about six years, and considering as well that a star programmer becomes more valuable every day for up to forty years, the CA programmer makes and earns far more. Charles: "You've got to pay them—and pay them well. When you get a dedicated guy, pay him twice as much, because you can eliminate three other people."

Charles' dictum for success in writing software, famous within the industry—when a group of five programmers can't develop a piece of software, remove the two weakest—is based on a simple idea: good is an obstacle to great. But it won't work unless you have the great.

VIII. Ranking

Discovering who is most valuable is the key to reorg. CA's process goes head to head with U.S. industrial norms. American companies are very good at laying off 20 percent of the cleaning staff, six secretaries, and four people in the mailroom but never seem to get around to slamming the door on incompetent vice presidents, to say nothing of chairmen. American business is structured for stability, not performance. Once you structure for performance, it becomes immediately clear that a way must be found to discover which employees perform best. Sure, most companies go through a rote, ubiquitous employee evaluation, where on a one-to-five continuum everyone turns out to be a three. Great, but how do you know which threes are the best threes? You don't. At CA, employees are ranked: she is number one in this group; he is number two; he is number three, and on down. At CA, employees are ranked against each other. There can be no other meaning for best. Charles: "And always be bluntly, brutally honest with your people. You screw up, I tell you you screwed up. 'Now, tell me how we're going to do it so next time we don't have this problem, and what did we learn from this?' Or it could be, 'OK, you did great, kid. You did great. I can't believe you did it, I didn't think you could, but you did great.' Tell them! If you don't tell them how you feel, how are you going to expect anything from them? It's not fair."

These are initially difficult decisions, but once made, they provide the raw material for positive decision making on a grand scale. The decision making concerns people: who are the best people for the most important jobs?

IX. Human Nature

Even at CA there is resistance to ranking. Managers are often reluctant to make hard decisions about employees with whom they work closely in a nonauthoritarian environment. Even at CA, people feel uncomfortable with making comparative judgments about other people. Charles: "I rank them, I tell them. Yeah, and if you screw up, I'll put you in the penalty box for a while. I'll tell you you screwed up and that's why you're there. Now, learn something while you're there. And if you don't like it, leave—because CA doesn't need you and you don't need CA. You're talented, go somewhere else where you love it. You don't think we love you, but I'm going to tell you exactly where you stand. I don't think there's anything wrong with that. I tell people to treat their people the same way. But here's where even we get wishy-washy, back and forth. Someone says, 'This person is the worst person I ever had.' Then he says, 'He is probably the best employee I ever had.' Come on, you said he's bad—he's bad. But now suddenly he's the best? Come on, these cancel each other out. This is a meaningless piece of bull, this report. 'Why'd you bother putting anything down there in the first place? Oh yeah, you've got to check off because you have to fill out the form, but that's not the purpose of that form. The form wasn't meant to be filled out so that everybody's file has this form signed by a manager. That's not the purpose of it. The purpose was for you to face the issue of telling your person where he stands in your organization.' This is a long story at CA. We did it before and tried every which way, and every time I got myself into problems. They always tell you ranking demoralizes. So I said, 'OK, fine, don't rank anybody, guys. Just write on your form everything you think the guy can improve on, nothing about how good he is.' They couldn't do that either because it was all so negative. So I finally said, 'No way, we are going back to ranking everyone and that's it.' Whether it's one or two on the rank, OK, that's very subjective and perhaps depends on the mood and perhaps depends on a personal relationship. So they asked not to have to rank the top third. I said, 'You don't have to rank the top third. Fine, don't write it.' So then the bottom two-thirds get ranked and the top third gets ranked too, but it's not in their file so it's not their problem. The beginning of the end, because they'll bastardize it and the following year they'll say, 'Well, we don't want to rank them this way,' and I'll say, 'Very well, we're going back to ranking everyone.' That's all. I mean, we'll give them their shot, they're heard. If it doesn't work, enough managers will say, 'Charles, it worked better before.' Bingo, we're back to the way it was."

The pyramidal company may be inefficient, static, and doomed to eventual failure, but stiff hierarchies have one great advantage for most people. They are comfortable. Tony: "We reshuffle the deck every year. Look at Arnie's history here, multiple jobs, double duty. When people at other companies see the kind of changes and reshuffling that goes on at CA, they think, *Watch out, it indicates a down quarter.* But for us it's part of the atmosphere created here. People who thrive in the culture do very well. They don't have to wait for their boss to die. But there's a negative side: there are people who are not comfortable with that. Typically in other companies there are well-defined career paths—junior programmer, senior programmer, group leader, manager, assistant VP with larger office, then VP with a private secretary. These kinds of people can feel uncomfortable here. They can't be sure where they're going to be five years from now." It is just those people that Charles Wang does not want leading CA.

X. Reorg

The military is the model for the twentieth-century corporate hierarchy. Yet even this most rigid of pyramids breaks down when a sluggish peacetime army is exposed to combat. Say a sergeant is killed: a weak lieutenant will choose the replacement from among the corporals only; a strong officer will choose from among all the available personnel. If the best man is a buck private who has shown courage, skill, and an appetite for overcoming challenge, so be it. In a society at war, military management rapidly becomes more efficient than civilian management. It must.

The Israel Defense Forces is the army most often cited as the best pound-for-pound fighting organization in the world. Yet the same talent pool exists in Israeli business, which is an inefficient, uncreative, deeply featherbedded mess. Why the disparity? For half a century Israel's army has been constantly at war. The need for fresh leadership is so high a priority that even in the lulls between wars, potential star officers are constantly being plucked out of the herd and tagged for advancement. Every commanding officer in the IDF is himself judged on his own ability to discover, develop, and motivate the best men.

Keeping a corporation on this kind of war footing is all but impossible: corporate sergeants are rarely killed in action. More often they themselves help kill the company through their inaction. In order to do more than just enough, they must be motivated. In most U.S. companies, the motivation is threefold: status, perks, and cash—usually in that order. But if this works, it probably only manages to avert an even worse situation, in which, as under communism, no one is motivated at all. In a company where the best have as much chance to rocket ahead as the next-best, what advantage can there possibly be in doing any more than your job passingly well, kowtowing to your boss, and watching your ass? Only by ranking personnel can the best be assured of moving ahead.

And only through ranking can Charles Wang manage a company as big as CA (now nearly eight thousand people), as various (CA develops, sells, and services hundreds of software products), as spread out (with well over a hundred principal offices in the United States and around the world), and as dynamic. Though Charles has an elephantine memory for people who work at CA, not even Dumbo himself could know enough about each on a current basis: Charles depends on fresh updates from others down the line. With this knowledge he and a small group of managers can go about their job, which is to decide what the company should be doing, where it should be going, and how fast. Without this knowledge the process could not succeed.

XI. Zero-Based Thinking

Reorg could not be more simple. Because the company's productive assets are people, not machinery, CA's only constraint in reinventing the system to use them most effectively is the current product base, which must still be sold and supported. Charles calls this "zero-based thinking," as against zero-based budgeting. The latter assumes the corporation is already doing the right thing, while the former determines what the corporation should be doing and only then begins to allocate resources. Zero-based thinking is actually start-up thinking, but with none of the constraints: a functioning company is already in place, replete with product line, established clientele, dependable suppliers, to say nothing of solid credit, positive cash flow, money in the bank, and trustworthy personnel. So why change it?

The very idea flies in the face of both received business wisdom and what is thought to be common sense. A system that works should be allowed to keep working, no? Yes, and the system that works at CA is reorganization. Its stability is in change. For CA to become a highly rigid pyramid would be to destroy the system that has produced so much industrial wealth.

Thus freed from having to build CA according to its arrayed assets, Charles is able to redeploy his assets to work toward new goals: determining where CA should be going, both in the next year and, because software development takes time, over many years; determining which of the company's products have just about reached maximum penetration of their markets, and how these products can be enhanced and combined with other products to offer the advantages of a superproduct; determining which new markets the company should be in (both in terms of products and geography—about half of CA revenues derives from its international operations); determining what its competitors are likely to be doing (as CA expands its base of products, it expands its base of competitors); and finally, determining the priorities of all of these. On the other side of the blackboard, he lists his assets: people. Charles: "What I do is write my priorities. Let's say I redo a development area. I start off by saying I have nothing. What's my most important product, what's my strategy in this area? I always ask myself, *Why are we marketing this product?* We have a sort product, CA-Sort. *Why does one use a sorting product?* And I'll start to ask the questions, go through the process: 'OK, why do we do this? Is there a future to this?' Maybe we shouldn't be investing as much into it. Or what is the optimum we can invest? What do we have to do next year, guys, to keep the sorting market just the way it is, assuming no new sales? What would it take to do that? You say, 'Half-time one person will do fine.' OK, that's one. Then we go through all the different product areas, and let's say in one specific area we go through it and say, 'What is our problem?' 'Well, support there is bad.' 'Why?' 'Well, people are not being trained—bad manager there.' 'OK, let's address that issue.' Then on the other side of the board, I start to put down who are my key players in this. I put them all down. Then when you look up, you say, 'Of course, it's so simple. The thing that has the highest priority, you put your best people on it.' I always say, 'Well, if you started a company just to produce products and support products in this area, not sell them, who would you hire first in all this mess? Who would you say is your number one guy you'd want right next to you?' If they ask me this and I'm starting up, I say I want Russ. OK, that's my boy, Russ. Why? Because Russ can do so many things, he has this multitalented thing that he can help me with. Whatever reason. 'So who is yours?' We go through it. 'Well, why are you asking for this guy?' The process, the process—you go through it and through it and through it, until finally you look at it and you've got everybody right. All the priorities are right. And you've got the people, who your stars are. Then you start matching them up. Your number one star should go to your number one priority. Not very complicated.''

Reorg time can be a difficult period for CA personnel. People become easily attached to their jobs, their current objectives, the view from their chair. There is also fear that one's star may have ceased rising. Charles: "Bullshitting is what does it, bullshitting. Cover-your-ass bullshit. That's it. If you make a mistake, say, 'I made a mistake.' And I always ask the same next question, 'OK, guys, what did we learn from this thing?' I don't care so much what the result is. I want the process. Once the process is right, the substance follows. Everything else comes out of it. You know, it's like what Confucius says: 'Give a guy a fish, feed him for a day. Teach him how to fish, feed him for life.' The process. We worry more about the process of the thing, how it gets done, not just what gets done. But the process keeps changing—it's a living thing almost—because the market changes. As we change inside, the variables change, so we change. So the person who can really thrive is the person who can adjust to change and can overcome these problems. The guy who gets fired is someone who can't adjust to it and makes a mistake and then spends all his time convincing others that it's really not his mistake, it's somebody else's—and it gets everybody into an uproar. He's gone. He is unhappy, so we part ways."

Because CA encourages its people to feel the sky is the limit, even a temporary setback or minor dressing down can cause bitterness, even trauma. On many occasions subordinates have become responsible for their former managers, though this is sweetened somewhat by the ex-manager's paycheck remaining unchanged. Outside of the sales area, which is commission based, salary cuts don't happen. This allows a good deal of leeway for human problems: X was going through a divorce; Y was simply unsuited to marketing; Z couldn't get along with his manager. Lateral shifts can take place, allowing a second chance. People are assets that can learn. But *can learn* doesn't necessarily mean *will learn*. A third chance is unlikely.

Moving people around this way—shuffling the deck, as Tony likes to call it—reinvigorates the company and moves the right people into the new positions that Charles has determined are right. The process would, however, be all but impossible were CA structured like most American companies. Pyramids, the most stubbornly unbudgeable of all structures, tend to crumble when you remove any part but the top, which is why change in corporate America, when it happens at all, is a change at the top. And about as consequential.

Part Two:

Operation

I. Inner/Outer Management

At CA there is no top. There is a center. The corporate structure, if such a term can be used at all, is not a pyramid but a complex and ever-shifting set of solar systems whose basic unit is the orbit. Each of these systems is a collection of people—some close in, some further out—circling a common hub in their own individual three-dimensional orbits, each with its own direction. Likewise, all the systems orbit a central hub. It follows then that there is no higher and lower management at CA, only inner and outer management, with other orbits of management radiating from there. Have a look at the following diagrams: Diagram 1 is corporate America. We see it in business, the armed forces, government, even education. Straight vanilla. All decision making derives from the top. The direction of the company is clear; after all, a pyramid is just an arrow frozen in stone. Structurally,

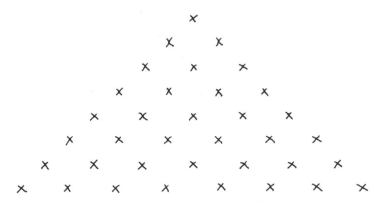

Diagram 1

the function of all building blocks is to support the one block at the top, the boss.

There are only two possible ways to change such a structure: reduction of the outer surfaces (like clerical help, which is why cutbacks and layoffs rarely affect those blocks most closely supporting the apex) and total ruin, either through outright demolition or the irremediable abuse of time. The pyramid is otherwise incapable of change, often surviving its own functionality. Mexico and Egypt are full of these magnificent hulks, with no significance other than as a monumental reminder that what once served an important function is without life—a memorial to vision, perhaps, but nothing more. If CA had ever started building itself this way, construction was halted early on.

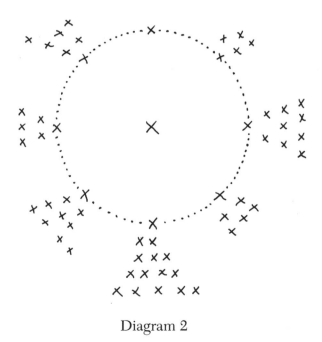

Diagram 2

Diagram 2 is CA on its way, with Charles at the center of a circle of trusted colleagues, each happily managing a function of the company: development, marketing, sales, administration, finance, international, or whatever else was thought important enough at any given time to be so singled out. Notice that this is not a wheel at all, but something more like a Roman candle, with the force of management exploding out from the center to an ever-receding collection of the same kind of rigid structures CA was earlier trying to escape. True, Charles and his circle are able to communicate like crazy, but everyone else is frozen out into the farthest reaches of Pyramidville.

This is CA in the full flower of its adolesence, stuck with the disadvantages of both childhood (the pyramid) and adulthood (the circle) and benefiting from neither. (Warning: do not try to roll this thing forward. Its prongs will simply snap off, probably out of frustration.)

Yes, the structure encourages group interaction at the hub, but even members of the hub group are more or less cut off from access to areas of responsibility not specifically their own. Say the head of marketing wants to talk to someone in development. She's still got to go through the head of development and, if the person she needs is pretty far down on the development pyramid, through a lot of other managers as well. Worst of all, the people who really know everything, the people in the field or those actually doing the development or the selling, are still locked away at the base of the pyramid. In order for a programming person to hear from marketing that there is demand for an enhancement of some piece of software, the message must be relayed through many stations down to the hub and back out again. As in any other pyramid, the stuff and guts are unseen,

69

unknown, and blindly unable to affect direction, which of necessity is controlled from the apex.

In one sense, a pure case of the donkey (diagram 1) beats the mule (diagram 2). Mules are OK for pulling weight. Just don't expect to breed them for flexibility, say, or shorter ears: mules are sterile. In marrying the circle to the pyramid, each manages neatly to cancel the other out. Diagrams 3a and 3b are more like it. In the first—a simplified and rather static version of the second—notice that groups of people move in orbit around the central hub. This calls to mind Baron George-Eugène Haussmann's breakthrough in the nineteenth-century restructuring of Paris. The French capital was a mess of tiny intersecting streets before this brilliant engineer cut broad boulevards across and around the city. The advantages are obvious. By radiating streets from a central hub, distances are vastly reduced, and vistas are opened up in all directions. This is why Paris is the world's greatest city for tourists on foot.

City planning, however, is one dimensional, so look at 3b. Not only are there many more orbits, but planets in each group spin in different directions in three dimensions, and each individual planet turns as well on its own axis. There is infinite overlap. These spheres merely look like they are colliding: think not of planets, which tend to crash nastily on contact, but of lights, which, when they cross in the interplay of expressed ideas, increase in brilliance. Diagram 3b more accurately reflects today's CA—or what it is becoming, because the process never seems to end.

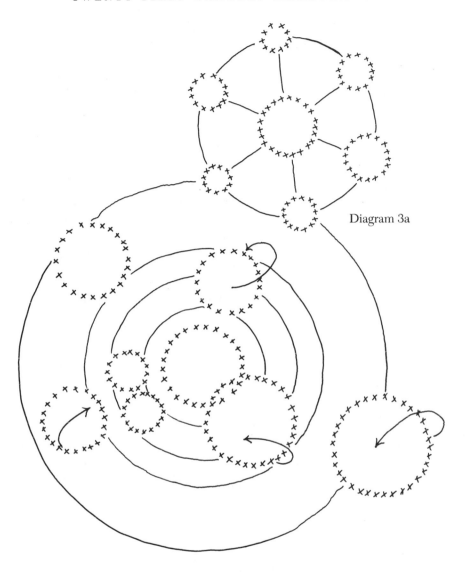

Diagram 3a

Diagram 3b

II. Inner Management

Consider this the astronomic version of CA, with Charles and Tony, Sanjay, Arnie, and several others at the center. Though Charles will ultimately make final decisions on technology and marketing, Sanjay shares much authority in these fields, so that often Charles will sit through the beginning of a meeting and Sanjay will sit through the end. Sanjay: "People who like job descriptions wouldn't like my job. And they wouldn't like CA. I am kind of liaison to a lot of clients, so I spend a lot of time talking to them. I'm enough business and enough technical where I can deal with this. Same thing in sales. I get involved in planning for sales. Planning financials for an acquisition. Product development. Almost everything that falls off Charles' desk falls onto mine. CA management is just incredibly hands-on—so hands-on it's unbelievable. But not all the guys at the top can have their hands everywhere. OK, so what do we do? You can say we're collectively one body with lots of arms, lots of fingers. So if I can be an extension of Charles, he has ten more fingers. If Charles can be an extension of me, I get ten more fingers. Very often Charles and I don't go to the same thing, we go to different meetings, but the trick is when we get back together we kind of unload on each other and say, 'OK, here's what's going on.' A by-product of what we do is travel together, and that's a good time to get caught up on, say, what's going on maybe in product strategy. Here on Long Island, if Charles is away, I can deal with it, if I'm away Charles can deal with it. That way no one person becomes a bottleneck." **Toward eve-**

ning they'll hash out the day in Tony's office, where Tony will wonder what benefit the earlier meeting's conclusions bring to CA. Tony: "We tend to discuss things a lot among ourselves. Decisions are made on a group basis, as opposed to an individual basis. There's a group dynamic, despite the sense that decisions are made mainly by Charles. Because we're always part of the group. For example, let's say all decisions are made by Charles after he has taken in what everyone thinks. He may show where he's heading, but in reality I'm sure he feels that way only after a bunch of people come in and he gets to hear their views. If the consensus in a meeting is against an acquisition and he's obviously hot for this deal, within the senior group most would still say no. My recollection is if everyone is against something, Charles probably won't do it." Typically, Arnie suggests ways to get around the problems while retaining the benefits. No less typically, Charles suggests another way around them. Russ wanders in to note soberly that the key element is time, because it may take as long as four months to complete the step-by-step process of developing this particular enhancement to an existing program, preparing the support, and publishing the collateral information. So there is some question when it can be ready for market.

Sanjay says that's a shame, because short-term there is nothing like it on the market, and long-term it adds value to CA's existing programs by tying them together around a graphics base. But it should be brought out in time to be offered as an extra-cost option with the scheduled release of the program's new version, which is a matter of forty-five days.

No one has mentioned price, but Charles is scribbling numbers on the scratch pad on his lap. He is figuring out the gross revenue value of the enhancement if it can be produced from start to finish within forty-five days.

Russ whistles softly. He'll have to ask Nancy if three really fast programmers can be shifted from what they're doing for a month. Arnie says casually that that's a good idea, because Jim Berryhill, who runs sales in the Southeast, has already signed up four banks, a hospital, and the supervisor's office of a large county in Florida. They want the product, but only with the enhancement. "Sort of a presold trial balloon," Arnie says. Tony, who is blessed with expressive eyes, rolls them. Charles: "I'm very private with my private life, socialize very, very little. Just with several people here. Tony. Arnie. Michael Picker, Paul Lancey. Sanjay. Russ. Basketball players. We call ourselves the Dumpling Gang." **An hour later they are playing basketball at Charles' house.** Russ: "When I hire someone I'm looking to see if this person seems to be nuts in terms of the way we work and goes for it as a competitor. And that's a big part of it. A lot of us are competitive. We have a weekly basketball game, and we're nuts. We go crazy. I got a thumb I can't bend now for a month because we were playing basketball, but I've been playing every week anyway. Same game, Charles got his thumb hurt too. Same game. Both of us with thumbs like this. We are maniacs. When we go at each other, it's the most competitive experience you've ever seen. We go for it. It's like we're playing for our life." **Charles asks Michael Picker, who early in his career at CA managed to break Charles' nose in a basketball game, if the documentation can be printed and packaged within a week, after support writes it in a month in tandem with development, which is writing the program at the same time.** Tony does the thing with his eyes. Mike says, "Why not?" Russ: "You know you've gotta, you've

74

gotta get the job done. You know that, and you get it done regardless of how you get it done. You get it done."

The next morning Russ meets with Nancy, who takes on responsibility for getting two programmers working. Nancy: "You don't need three." Don Osley, senior vice president, research and development, who sits next door, cuts short his vacation to start working up the support. Don: "I've found a home here— if they need it, I'll empty garbage cans." Marketing is already designing literature for sales, which is working up a commission schedule, which has to be printed. Bing Wen, who runs printing, puts in another sixteen-hour day. The process continues through every orbit of CA. Charles: "You want to know how I make decisions, but it's not how—it's who. I tell myself, Sanjay, Arnie. I talk to them." Basketball is optional.

III. Paperless Office

Throughout this entire procedure, not one memo has been written. Nancy: "I came in to see Arnie about a specific problem, and everyone else was sitting there eating lunch. So we ended up all talking about it, and then we talked about some other things. While you're there, you take care of other things. You don't wait."

For those of us who naively believed the promise that computers would one day generate the paperless office, this is all the more remarkable. In millions of businesses around the world, the computer is now being used to generate mountains of memos, cubic acres of agreements, caverns of checklists. Indeed, together with its dumb brothers, the fax and the copy machine, the computer caused American usage of office paper in 1990 to surge to 155 percent of the 1980 level. Yet CA, which is so intimately involved with almost every aspect of American business—its software is standard at 475 companies on the Forbes and Fortune 500's—can't be bothered with the very memos that are the lifeblood of U.S. corporate existence and without which its entire organic structure would collapse. Russ: "Come on, we have a structure. Sure, it's not all that rigid, you know, and exactly what two people with the same title do or don't do varies with the circumstance. What we have is a reporting structure—people who work for me, who I work for. Superproduct-owners have product-owners working for them. Product-owners have development managers and support managers. I mean, we do

76

have a structure. We do have org charts. Charles used to maintain them, and now Don Osley does, and Nancy. Everything's on-line, on the computer. Everyone's on the charts, but charts are charts and people are people."

At CA memos have been replaced by brief face-to-face discussions and an oral OK. Russ: "I mean, it's not so structured in the sense that I'll think nothing of bypassing the product-owner and going directly to a development leader to find out: 'Hey, what's going on? This product's screwed up, let's find out why'—you know? That's the way we work. We don't necessarily follow protocol or this or that and, you know, worry about hurting people's feelings. You do what you have to do." **Two people talking together in a corridor.** Peter A. Schwartz, chief financial officer: "For chrissakes, my family's more structured than this company."

Even something as important as a major licensing agreement will go out with one lonely signature on the CA side, while the client side is a veritable follow-the-dots of vice-presidential sign-offs: VP contracts, VP legal, VP purchasing, VP data center, VP systems, VP administration, VP finance, VP accounting, VP who knows? Alec Wilson, senior vice president: "Do you want to see a contract? It's a licensing agreement. Here's my name on one side and twelve signatures on the other side. Twelve. What you have to understand is that I once worked for that company. They were men in empty suits then, and they haven't changed. They don't want to make decisions. Twelve signatures. This way, they're all safe." **Which is not to say that CA eschews documentation. CA is a bear for backing up its software at every stage of development, a real departure in an industry where Charles was once unable to acquire a well-**

known word-processing package because the company that wanted to sell it had misplaced the code to its own software. To find it, the prospective seller eventually had to buy a second company started by a former employee who happened to have a copy of the code.

CA's approach is not quick and dirty, however. It is more like quick and briefly noted. Just as Tony insists the company balance its radical operational side with the kind of highly conservative financial structure that in 1991 held $250 million in cash, Charles knows CA's very informality demands an accurate and completely up-to-the-minute record of what is going on. Charles: "Look, here's the whole deal of what went on today. Half a sheet of paper. This is it. This is the whole deal. I wrote it all down. To buy a product. This is it. I know exactly what everything on here is. This is the whole plan. This is to buy a product, and it comes out to two hundred fifty thousand dollars right here, plus royalties of eight percent. OK? Minimum of a hundred thousand first year. Based on what kind of study, what kind of planning? Based on my talking to the guy, and this is it. This is the whole summary of the whole plan. Of what we're going to do. We all agreed to the terms." This is documentation that concerns CA and the world, not who said what inside CA.

Yet even within the company, some form of record keeping is necessary because things move so fast. So Charles encourages his people to do what he does, keep a black-and-white hardbound school-kid's notebook and jot down what they've done, what they've agreed to do, what they expect done. Charles likes the notebooks for the same reason teachers do: when you've blotted your copybook, you can't tear the leaf out without releasing a trail of loose pages in the rest of the notebook. Message: you can't escape the consequences of what you do, so try to do it right.

This informal record keeping has a hidden plus: it frees up time for operations. Without the need to constantly keep up the flow of memos detailing plans for operations or memos summarizing decisions or memos acknowledging receipt of memos, CA has made fast response the rule, not the exception. When John J. ("Jay") Callanan, senior vice president for operations, feels he needs an OK on part of the $180 million in contracts CA has let for the building of its new corporate headquarters, the last thing he will do is write a memo. Jay: "The people in this company spend their time and effort operating the business, not keeping themselves from operating it with a bureaucratic approval process that requires voluminous weekly and monthly reports and quarterly reports and quarterly presentations and slide presentations—all of which requires enormous preparation time, enormous presentation time." He merely walks thirty feet down the hall to Tony's office. Jay: "Which is time you're not doing business. I've worked for GE and Boeing, companies so restrictive in terms of your job responsibility, with impossible limitations and checks and balances. Here there's an element of trust in your judgment that permits you to move at great speed to discharge your responsibility. But it goes further. CA encourages you to have an ever-increasing amount of elasticity, both in terms of responsibility and judgment. You're not only not stifled, you're encouraged to take on a variety of things and accept more and more responsibility. You have an increasing level of responsibility as long as you demonstrate all along that course that you exercise judgment properly and profitably. Here's this deal I just did for the data center in our new building. Last year I did a similar deal. Now I simply negotiated the same deal, tacked on two more months because we need that for the move, walked down the hall to Tony, and said, 'Here's the deal, it was so-and-so million last year, it's this-and-such million this year. It makes sense—here are the reasons. Will you please approve this purchase order and this invoice, and I intend to pay them Friday afternoon.' Then I walk across to Pete Schwartz and tell him, 'Pete, I need a check for this-and-such million by Friday.' Now look, I've been working with this supplier company for months, but all it takes internally is ten minutes with Tony and five with Pete Schwartz and it's on to the next thing." **No memo.** Jay: "In another company it would have taken weeks and months, preceded by the preparation of piles of documents, surveillance from legal and financial and operations, thirty-seven third-party overviews. This deal would have had so many different inputs it's unlikely it would ever have been concluded." **No appointment.** Jay: "But here it works because you have guys like Charles and Tony who are involved in the day-to-day operation of the business, who understand the nuances of the people who work for them and with them, who are able to color a Jay Callanan conversation and understand what he really said as opposed to what they heard him say. There's a trust in people, and if you demonstrate and continue to demonstrate that you are worthy of that trust, you continue to have that authority and responsibility." **No "cover your ass."** Jay: "And if you demonstrate that you're one of the guys here—and we have them—who runs in to find out whether he can go to the bathroom, then that becomes your area of authority and responsibility, the bathroom." **No sweat.**

IV. Outer Management

In the paperless office the only way to advance is to work well. Sending memos and making grand presentations—the appearance of working well—is just not an option at CA. Charles: "I want self-starters, not ass-kissers." The devices themselves, having been made unnecessary, do not exist. Jay: "There is a close enough dialogue between the people who run the business and the people who help them do that, so there is a frequent flow of information and understanding of what the work is. It helps that you have two guys involved here with an enormous capacity to understand. They're involved on a continuing basis. I can go down and talk to Charles right now about a federal customer, U.S. Customs, and he'll have a pretty good idea because he would have met U.S. Customs executives at some prior chief information officer conference, where there is senior management presence by CA all the time. There is a remarkable hands-on understanding of what each piece of the business is doing or attempting to do." People predisposed to the frippery of memos quickly find themselves on the street.

For those prepared for the challenge of a nonstructured or continually restructured environment, there is no orderly progression along a predetermined course from spear carrier to commanding general. Bob Toth, senior vice president, sales: "When I had the signing authority, even when I got a fair amount of authority—for signing contracts, say, or writing something off the books of the company, or large credits—I mean someone may come and ask me or challenge me later. I found that even when I was challenged—because I made some good decisions and some bad ones too—they have always encouraged me to keep making decisions, not to stop. Even if I made a bad one." **In fact, there are no spear carriers, but merely people whose management responsibilities are more constrained than others.** Bob: "What happens when you make a bad one? You feel the bumps. I have been challenged and lost. And maybe I had to walk away with my tail between my legs." **But not permanently.** Bob: "At one point some responsibility was taken away from me because they thought I was challenging things too much or that I was in the way versus helping the situation." **Because if you know your place, if everyone knows his or her place, the whole operation will never move forward.** Bob: "Which was interesting, because in that particular case they came back to me, Charles and Tony, and said, 'You were probably right, we should have listened to you.'" **Because whatever doesn't change is dead.** Charles: "Yeah, we make mistakes all the time. So correct and go on. No big deal."

Audacity, the principal ingredient in most informal and thus evolving organizations, is nowhere more evident than in guerrilla warfare, which carries not knowing your place to the ultimate. Yet in every situation where guerrilla forces have been victorious because of the aggressiveness of local commanders—from colonial America to modern-day China, Algeria, Cuba—the next stage is so woefully predictable it has become a cliché: a hierarchy is formed, frozen in time, and fixed in place. While the guerrilla struggle encouraged new leadership, from independence day forward any attempt on the part of new or young

individuals to take responsibility even at the lowest level is usually doomed to failure, if not torture and death. Nothing records this more clearly than newspaper photographs, aging year by year, of the same figures smiling confidently as early success turns to institutionalized failure. But petrified elites are not limited to Third World nations: the world over, annual reports of large corporations march us past the same forced smiles frozen on the same aging faces.

Clearly such management sclerosis is caused by two breakdowns: (1) an unwillingness among those above to accept the challenge of new ideas, and (2) a concomitant fear among those below of offering them. When the Chinese say that the nail that sticks up will be beaten down, they describe any command society where all decisions not made at the top are a threat. The term *concomitant fear* is not meant to blame those below, who naturally have an interest in rising to the top. It is those above we must blame: they instill the fear. As the proverb has it, the fish stinks from the head.

But it doesn't have to stink at all. In providing open pathways for those who demonstrate management skill, leadership, and responsibility, CA has changed the rules of the game. How? By reducing the level of nonmanagers at CA to near zero: nearly everyone at CA manages something. By managing something, each employee can be judged against the performance of others. Reuven Battat, senior vice president, research and development: "When I worked at IBM, the system was everyone was evaluated, yes, but not against others. You got a number, from one to five, with one being the best and five meaning you'd be under strong pressure to leave the company. Until recently, IBM didn't fire, so instead you'd be offered relocation to someplace you didn't want to go. But when you evaluate this method, which seems so logical, you get a funny result: everybody turns out to be a two or three. So how can you really distinguish between people? You have a spot to fill, a new responsibility for someone—but you can't choose the someone. At CA you can choose the someone. You can see it, like a pathway, very clear." **In providing this pathway to recognition, CA is one of the few large American corporations that has actively sought to promote from the lowest level and not merely from some executive training ground.** A very senior executive: "I had a great administrative assistant, but for personal reasons she had to leave. Over the years I've had a lot. Most are still with the company, doing other things at various levels. So here I am needing another, and I asked personnel who would be good, and interviewed several. I thought I knew the job. This woman I hired had it down cold in a week. Then she reorganized it the way it should have been done. Then she started taking on some of the routine work I have to do— budget approvals, when it's more or less cut and dry—and then she started explaining to me areas that might need looking at. A month into the job and she sees problems that even I missed or didn't have time to handle. I'd say, 'Handle it.' And she would. Then she's handling problems that are similar, I mean on her own. She is now doing twenty-five percent of my job, which leaves me enough time to concentrate on the rest of it. When I'm away, she's making decisions instead of just collecting them and saving them for me. The trouble is, I'm going to lose her because I can't keep her down. One day she will probably be a vice president."

Consider: fully half the administrative assistant slots at CA have produced managers—those promoted to supervisory capacity at

least once—and half of these have been repromoted. The secretarial/clerical/admin pool, corporate America's pink-collar sink trap, has at CA become a source for middle and higher executives, everything from account managers to client-base administrators to assistant vice presidents and even one vice president. Elaine Quigley, vice president for administration: "I was hired to run the travel at CA, and after about a year it was determined they were going to let the travel go back out to the travel agency. At that time there was no job for me because I was a travel agent. Tony said to me, 'Why don't you work on some special projects for me, then maybe we'll find a spot.' So I did a whole bunch of odd things, and then I guess I worked for telecommunications and then purchasing. Administration was vacant up here—there was nothing here. So I developed it into all this. I actually made a one-person role about a hundred people, which saves a great deal of money. We now do everything we can in-house."

Of course there are those on both the administrative and technical sides who remain unwilling to accept the challenge of management responsibility. Not only are they not stigmatized at CA, but in a company where upward (or inward, toward-the-center) mobility is the norm, such people are treasured. They are the islands of stability in a sea of change. Nancy: "There's this Product Integration Group—Pigs. They're completely unmanaged. They provide tools to enhance all the other products and help to integrate them. The requirements come from the product groups, who say, 'We need something that would do this. Do the architecture.' They're all individualists, very quirky, talented but quirky. So it's a growth path for those technicians who are ambitious but don't want to manage." That at least *somebody's* role doesn't change every month must be great solace for any dispirited personnel managers who read this book.

Though they might wish to quit reading here. In a company where the dictatorship of the job description has been overthrown by enthusiastic and systematic encouragement of growth and change, the role of CA's personnel department is, by Western corporate standards, unrecognizable.

Don't expect a lot of mourners.

Using the best pseudoscientific methods—everything from misapplied Rorschach testing to the kind of objective interviewing that assigns grades to posture, grooming, and marital status—the prototypical American corporate personnel manager actually runs his company, especially if we take as a given that employees are any corporation's unique value-adding asset. This great equalizer hires (according to elaborate technical specifications that permit human beings all the predictability of probed jellyfish), determines standards for promotion (curiously uniform, as though people are), and often even fires (especially when employees show signs of being in some way unique). Russ: "You need quality people, you need good management directing them, and in both cases you get a lot of people, especially in development but not exclusively, who are what you'd call prima donnas. It's not always the case, but very often it seems that the more talented people tend to be real individuals. It's a big management challenge to deal with a lot of different and sometimes difficult personalities. But you know, that's life: people are interesting." Authority without accountability? Yes, but at least this approach does one thing well: it maintains the status quo—hell, the formula worked before, so let's keep doing it until the company closes. By its nature, this approach can contribute nothing to growth in a world where the rate of change is compounded daily. Yet the debility is so ingrained in the system that it is all but invisible until we look at a situation where the great god personnel has been toppled.

At CA, hiring and firing decisions are made by those who must live and work with the employee and his or her functionality. Russ: "When you have to make changes, the immediate superior makes the changes, or it would be discussed at a higher level, escalated. For instance, if Hank Heidler in Princeton, who's in charge of systems software, wasn't happy with one of his main people, he would go talk to Nancy, or to me and Nancy, and we'd sit down and talk about it. 'Let's discuss this guy. Why is he screwing up? Is this for him?' Basically, personality analysis. Especially if it's a change at a very high level, it would get escalated, but a more minor change Hank wouldn't discuss with Nancy. Certainly the change would be made by the people involved, no one else." **Period.** Russ: "Everyone has their own personality. Charles has his personality, I have my personality—we all have different personalities, but it's the same philosophy that we all follow. We all work in a dynamic mode. There are going to be changes, in products, in personnel, in the market, in everything. You've got to expect it. Because we're never going to be satisfied with what we've got. We're always going to want more, and to get more we've got to make changes. We have to be ready for the dynamics of that. My personality is such that I like changes. I mean, some people want to live in the same house their whole life. Not me. I like to move, I like to move. And a lot of people here are like that. They have to be because change is a constant." Where change is a constant, the role of personnel is passive. In a word: scorekeeping.

So effectively is personnel removed from managing the playing field that formal credentials (indeed the entire process of earning them and showing them off) become irrelevant. A position in marketing must be filled? In any sensible corporation the replacement would need a background in marketing. But how sensible is this in a company where a marketing manager has just moved over from development, her deputy has a degree in accountancy, and his principal administrator was hired eight months before as a graphic artist but moved over when the former admin went into sales? Yes, there are people who are good at only one thing, and others who are simply not good enough at others. But marketing is a lot like carpentry, acting, piloting a plane, sex: once you learn the basic moves, only your skill, imagination, and raw material limit your performance.

When all that matters is performance, many personnel-related necessities become superfluities: getting in at nine tends to become a quickly debased standard when the parking lot begins to fill before eight. And what can getting in at nine possibly mean to people who worked the night before until four in the morning?

Unless it has to do with missed deadlines or inconveniencing others, management by time-clock is an idea whose time has come and gone. (Yes, at CA, meetings do begin with a punctuality that might seem astounding in such a loose organization, but any less stringent a standard would not be tolerated by those who do arrive on time.) Is she at her desk? Probably not. She's already doing three jobs and taking on others. Does he work the long hours that helped make American productivity so much greater than that of European countries and which itself has now been eclipsed by the Japanese, the Koreans, and the Taiwanese? Does it matter? In a world where the quality of an idea and its execution matter, hours don't.

The fact is that some CA people do work long hours. (The standing joke at CA's former headquarters in Garden City, N.Y., was that its address—711 Stewart Avenue—was chosen deliberately to indicate the hours employees should put in.) But if long hours were the only ingredient for business success, the corporate skill of choice ought to be tolerance for Benzedrine. If CA people put in the hours, they do it—like Jay Callanan, who works from seven-thirty to seven-thirty—to get more done, not to impress someone else, because that someone else is simply too busy to notice. A middle manager: "I don't place value judgments on other people's wishes. You asked for my time, I make the time. Because you asked. Anybody who asks me to do anything, I do it. Fifty hours? You call fifty hours a long week? I would be happy with a fifty-hour week when I'm sick. Generally it's at least a twelve-hour day and then probably twelve over the weekend. But I do take all my vacations. I take my three weeks, whatever. You can be sure!"

Some CEOs—Microsoft's William Gates is famous for it—make it a point to leave messages at 2:00 A.M. in the electronic mail of subordinates. Whatever the intent, the effect is a chilling invitation to ruinous personal sacrifice.

Charles put in those hours in the early years. Lisa Mars, personnel manager: "When I first came here, Charles would be in at five-thirty in the morning and was still going strong at seven in the evening when I left. I felt like I was leaving at noon." But he obviously got to the point where he did not feel the need to run everything. Now he is in at eight or nine in the morning and out by six. Neither he nor anyone else in the company seems to understand the concept of the business lunch. No restaurants are booming around CA offices; these people eat either in the cafeteria or, quite commonly at every level of the company, at their desks. Tony once tried to have a working breakfast—brief, efficient, inexpensive—with CA's bankers at his neighborhood diner. The food was good, but hashing things out in thirty minutes over $1.25 hash browns discomfited the bankers.

Nothing is more indicative of CA's upending of American business tradition than the company's peculiar shortage of M.B.A.'s. Ask around at CA how many M.B.A.'s there are in the company, and the corridor wisdom is two or three. In fact there are ninety-three, but out of 4,328 North American employees this represents only 2 percent. (At IBM, where 40 percent of employees have higher degrees, there is some shyness about how many are M.B.A.'s, but a reasonable estimate is probably no less than 20 percent.) Of the dozen or so people with the highest authority at CA, only one has an M.B.A.: Peter A. Schwartz, who runs finance, where—arguably—an M.B.A. in finance can't do too much damage. Most of the other M.B.A.'s at CA are in hiding. Lisa: "When I got my M.B.A., Tony said, 'Good, now we can demote you.' " And for good reason.

Because performance is the only credential to be judged on the way to greater responsibility and higher pay, it must also be the only credential judged on the way down—or in terms appropriate to CA, out.

Consider the cases of three veteran CA people recently removed from very senior positions in the company—one from what might be called "near-absolute authority," that level of decision making where the only questions concerning the wisdom of a course of action might come from Charles. The other two were department heads: the first, a fine technician who could not handle the fairly routine administrative functions of his department; the second, a veteran CA manager who had felt so confident of his position that he repeatedly torpedoed decisions he did not like. The senior manager, having demonstrated the limits of his abilities by exceeding them—"a good number two, but that's all"—was moved elsewhere. The technician was moved back into development, where "he couldn't do any damage." The third, who was among CA's first dozen employees fifteen years before, was fired—but kept on the payroll for an extended period to cushion the blow. Each had been judged on performance, the quality of his decisions.

In any situation the ability to make good decisions is the key to success, but at CA this ability has an extra component, a subjective component. "Should this decision be made?" and "What should it be?" are joined at CA by a third question that would have no place in a traditional hierarchical structure where decision making is narrowly defined by areas of responsibility and position within the management pyramid. That question is: "Should I be the one making it?"

Though the quality of response to the first and second questions are important, at CA the third question comes first. Why? Arnie: "If you're not sure, ask. The most basic decision is, 'Is this something I should be deciding?' " Because a successful CA manager stretches his authority by increments. Arnie: "If

91

they make the right decision, they did it right. If they make the wrong decision, hopefully something was learned." **By demonstrating ability to choose the level of decision making and then making the right decision, decision-making authority grows.** Jay: "Whether I go for approval or not doesn't depend on whether I can support the rationale for the particular deal, because that's a given—it's whether I should be making the decision. Here I've got a three-point-six-million-dollar deal, big numbers, and I'm not prepared to make that deal happen without approval, so I discuss it. But if it's a twenty-five-thousand-dollar deal—or fifty thousand or a hundred and twenty thousand—these are decisions I make every day. On the other hand, there are decisions that I don't feel skilled to make that have nothing to do with money. I wouldn't pick a carpet selection for one hallway in the new CA headquarters building without going to Charles, because that's something that's personal to him. The company's personal to him, and the decor of that building is personal to him, and I know that I'd pick some drab gray color he'd go bananas about. So I know. I've worked with him for a period of time, and I have a feeling for the areas I should communicate on and the areas I don't have to. The carpeting decision isn't about money— it's about how Charles views the physical look of the company. Not how I do."

The question is not whether you can make the decision—the company is full of people who can take on responsibility in disparate areas—but whether the stretch is appropriate. In some cases the decision making is perfect if you bother no one else; in other cases, if you don't consult with people on levels higher, lower, or identical to yours, you are simply screwing the company.

In its early years CA hired an outsider to manage marketing—a rare occurrence, since nearly all post-entry-level hiring is internal or from acquired companies. Though a skilled and experienced executive, he was simply unable to work in perpetual twilight: he wanted to know where he stood, to make all marketing decisions on his own, even when these seriously impacted everything from finance to development to support to sales. Tony: "Very competent guy, but he had a hard time fitting in with our culture. He was just never comfortable with group dynamics, a group decision-making process—not one where the group made the decision, but where the group had to be involved. In this case, you can easily get to think you can't make any decisions. A guy like that would be much more comfortable as CEO of a traditional company, where if it's right, you get all the credit, or wrong, you get all the blame. Here, on the one hand, we're constantly trying to push down responsibility, but on the other hand, in the same culture we don't say, 'Here's North American sales for fiscal '92—you run it.' In the case of the man I'm talking about, he would have run it without chatting about it first. Now, if it works out . . . great. Nobody cares. But if there's a glitch in it, we're likely to say, 'Why did you do that?' "

Without a formal structure, the quality of decisions at CA depends on the quality of the people making them, not on the structure. Tony: "I myself get too much of 'Tony, what do you think of this?' That's just looking for confirmation. It's not discussion but a pat on the back, covering yourself. That doesn't help anyone. Yet the same person, who doesn't like to make decisions he should be making on his own, just did this, this thing right here on my desk, without asking me at all. Now this thing represents the entire company, and in my opinion it sucks. So this is someone who, the next time, will have to check with me. The problem with that is if every decision is handled that way, the same guy will never make a decision and I'll run out of eyes." **If the structure is stronger than the people, the company will never have the flexibility to grow and prosper.** Tony: "Look at Arnie. He's had as many as seventeen VPs reporting to him, all on the same level of responsibility. In order to manage it, he's got to delineate for them their level of responsibility. For instance, 'Grant discounts up to twenty-five percent, but not above.' Unfortunately, what you end up with is that not everyone is equal. Some with few rules do well. One sales manager uses his common sense and discounts where necessary. Another begins by figuring that everything starts with twenty-five percent off. You can have strict rules—'Only for seventeen percent of customers,' 'Only for deals over a hundred thousand dollars'—but then you get someone where the deal is ninety-nine thousand. Common sense says your judgment should be to give him the discount. But you run the risk of a manager saying, 'Sorry, we can't do it.' So we choose not to have these rigid rules. We could just as easily work that way, but we've chosen not to have so many stupid rules and details. Instead, we look for people who can make decisions using common sense, people who know when to make decisions on their own and when to consult. What it comes down to is people." **But finding good people is not easy.** Arnie: "I had a manager in a regional office who called me to say his secretary needed more money—she was going through a divorce and would otherwise have to leave for a job elsewhere at higher pay. According to the manager she was experienced and dedicated, and it would be a loss to the company if she left. So I asked how much she needed, he told me and I approved it.

Sometime later the manager was here on a visit, and I asked how the secretary was working out. He said, 'Oh, I convinced her to settle for half the raise—the other half I gave to another secretary in the office.' I said, 'The money was for a specific purpose. It wasn't your money to distribute. It's either the original secretary's money or CA's. Give it back.' And I gave him the choice of taking the money back from the second secretary or having the privilege of paying for it out of his own salary. Before coming to me, he should have found out how much the original secretary really needed. If she needed the full amount, how could he justify buying her on the cheap? We don't do that. Either she needed the money or she didn't. In the end I had a better idea of his ability to make decisions." **Authority must be earned.**

This is why good people at CA are given as much authority as they can handle. In fact, CA—which institutionalizes very little—absolutely enshrines this concept. Unwilling to tolerate a situation where many departments have a hand in a product, usually serially, but no one has either total control or total responsibility, Charles established a new function and spread it through the company: product-owner. Charles: "I don't think we one day woke up and said, 'Let's have product-owners,' and this brilliant lightning struck. I think it started off because there were things we were unhappy about in the company, where there was starting to be some finger pointing. Well, how do we overcome that? You can keep talking to the people and say, 'Don't finger point!' Or you can look at it as a question of priorities. So what do you do? You take their priorities and you put someone in charge of everybody and say he can set the priorities for his group. Well, you can call it anything you want. I call it someone who owns that area, owns a responsibility. He should have the wherewithal to worry about that responsibility. Then it's just a matter of do you have enough of these people, the good ones who can be product-owners. You know, we had a choice of calling them product-champions or product-owners, but champions seemed an added-on function. I champion something, but I don't really own it. It's not mine. I wanted them to feel it's theirs. It's their problems, it's their responsibility on everything that has to do with that product. So now if it's everything, if it's all-encompassing, what do you call yourself? I own the thing, so what do I call myself? An owner. Ahh, that's pretty good."

The product-owner became a product's chief executive officer. Sanjay: "Before the Uccel deal, there was product development from the guys that create the product. But with software there are bugs. So you have to fix them. And there is the support group. The support group used to work for sales. So you had development separate from sales and separate from support. What happened was that development would ship a product and then throw the responsibility over to support, who they didn't care about. But support had to support whatever development put out. It could be great or it could be terrible. If it broke, it was support's fault as far as development was concerned. But as far as support was concerned, it was development's fault because they put out a disaster to start with. Lots of finger pointing. Constantly. Constantly. Now, the organization we put together included development and support. They belonged together. The idea was, Give one person the accountability, give one person the authority—and make it all the same person. If he or she does well, tell him and take care of him. If he screws up, throw him out the door.

But give him the whole piece. Let him control his own destiny." **He owned it.** Sanjay: "In mid-1987 the first group to have development and support combined for a significant product line was put together. And that caused a lot of problems with some old-time CAers. The people who ran the support organization that was separate from development didn't like that. A number of them aren't here today. They left about a year later. They had lost the battle. So way back then Charles made that fundamental decision. Then, in early 1988, we went to this same concept, product-owner, throughout the company. The product-owner owned everything: development, support, quality assurance, technical writing, documentation, all of it together. And we restructured the entire company to do that." **Marketing, say, could no longer point a finger at development and claim it wasn't producing according to spec, because there was one person in charge.** Sanjay: "The entire company. Full responsibility, full accountability, full authority to go with it. And the rewards— and the punishment if you screwed up. That energized the company."

But as quickly as the system was set up, it began—inevitably—to change. Don Osley: "Product-owners who don't work out are no longer product-owners." **When product-owners couldn't do the job, products were orphaned, whole staffs left directionless. Charles then had two choices: (1) bring in a new candidate for a product that had already defeated others, or (2) move the product under the aegis of an already successful product-owner and have him supervise new product-owners as a superproduct-owner. Either way, product-ownership became a litmus test of managerial talent.** Russ: "You're running a product almost like running a business. You're totally responsible for the success or failure. It starts and ends with you. You've got total responsibility for getting the staff together, so you've got major people responsibilities. The people responsibility is huge in making sure individuals are motivated, directed properly, that you're all going in the same direction you want to be going in. And morale problems—all the stuff that comes with managing people. The product-owner has to make sure he's got the appropriate people, that he's got a team, and that the various responsibilities get met." **It was a form of neo-Darwinism.** Russ: "But not everyone's cut out for it. It's a new concept that we created here, and it really takes a well-rounded, versatile individual. It's got to be someone who's technical. He's got to understand the vision, where the product is, where it's going. Good with people. And support oriented. And development oriented. So we look from within and say, 'OK, who deserves this shot, who might be good?' And as talented as he or she may be, sometimes we find that this isn't a product-owner, so they might be best going back to what they were doing before, being a development leader for instance. He might be very good at that, but not a very good product-owner." **Natural selection.**

As the framework evolved, product-ownership took on a tensile strength within CA. Product-owners became responsible to superproduct-owners, who themselves became responsible to what can only be called mega–product-owners—the ultimate product-owner being Charles. Little wonder that the product-owners who succeeded took on the characteristics of Charles himself: extremely technical, marketing-sensitive managers who could motivate and lead people and who kept their eyes on the details while shaping the vision. With this sort of manager, a skein of "ownership" cut through the entire structure of development, marketing, and support at CA, functioning not as a wasteful alternative infrastructure but as the primary network of responsibility. Each product-owner is a mini-Charles, with bottom-line responsibility for coming through.

The CA dictum on management was now clearly in line with Charles' practice of removing two programmers from a project when five couldn't complete the job. Usually this would solve the problem. No? Then remove one or two more. What was important was the quality of the people who remained.

Product-owner became the ultimate in ranking—pass/fail with no safety net. Where, before, CA had had brilliant marketers, brilliant developers, brilliant financial controllers, and a half-dozen other categories of specific brilliance, a new personality began to emerge that eclipsed the others: brilliant product-owners. Quite often these individuals turned out to be less than brilliant in any one specific category, but their leadership and handling of responsibility had no parallel.

The job is complex, subtle and rigorously demanding. While the terms of engagement are brutally unforgiving (on the order of "succeed or 'bye"), the method of operation demands tact, foresight, and a familiarity with various individuals' needs and desires that verges on the intimate.

CA had found a way to put together the best combination of human talent at the level that counted most: the product level. This was simply a ramification of Charles' original logic. To make money, you need products; to get products, you need people—but you had to get the right people. They actually had to love working in such an exposed situation—virtually a guillotine—because if the blade doesn't fall, the same individual moves to a shady spot under an even larger blade, where he or she has total responsibility for a trickier product or a bigger one or a superproduct.

The principle of "succeed or 'bye" is so enshrined at CA that Tony's monthly Best Idea public notice always ends the same way, as does every internally communicated announcement of earnings, acquisitions, or personnel changes. "Remember," one assistant vice president told me, laughing in bemused embarrassment as he quoted the company's ubiquitous cheer-cum-admonishment, "that this is the most important day of the most important week of the most important month of the most important quarter in the history of CA." The AVP: "This is a classic line, our most important quote, to the point it's almost a joke. It's this process . . . that we're not going to dwell on past successes. That what we did great last month is nice but isn't going to be important and significant this month. The idea is: right now is what matters. We are not going to fall back on our laurels, we're not going to worry too much about where we are going to be in two years. What can we do with right now?"

What CA did with his bemused embarrassment was decide, on the basis of the work he was doing, that there were people already in the company—in this case a young woman who had shown promise—who could run the department better. She was given the department, the AVP—who understood CA's concept of total immediacy but saw it as "almost a joke"—was given the door.

For those who do take their work seriously, and can handle the responsibility, the payoff is as immediate as the penalty, and not all the payoff is in satisfaction.

100

V. You Give, You Get

What drives the corporation is usually not what drives the individuals on its payroll. To get everyone pulling in the same direction, the traditional corporation holds out a bunch of carrots—a package of highly structured financial and status rewards—while all but hidden behind its back is the stick of having these suddenly withdrawn. On both counts Computer Associates is radically different.

Not least because the stick—which isn't hidden at all—represents not loss of employment, but loss of job. Pardon? CA recognizes that all people are not uniformly good at all things. Reuven: "If somebody has a really good attitude, we find something for him—it's a big company. But if it's a severe attitude problem and it's affecting the people that work with him, it might reach termination." **Despite working hard, they may not work out.** Reuven: "But if he has the right attitude, he might just need training. Put him in the right job, and he usually works out." **Their potential may be better realized doing something else.** Paul Lancey, senior vice president: "I started here as an accountant, OK, and just barely was. I was mismatched as an accountant, because the reason I got to accountancy was that in college the courses were on the day I didn't play baseball. I probably became a good accountant here, and I became international controller. But I resigned that position because Charles said, 'Paul, you're playing out of position.' So I took a sales position—after being interna-

tional controller, started right at the bottom again as a salesman, became salesman of the year, regional manager, regional manager of the year, now this. All because he saw that
I was not in the right spot." **Titles and responsibilities may
change and may even seem to be less significant, but people are
willing to make the changes.** Bob: "There's a tremendous
sense of security here." **Their salary stays the same.** Arnie:
"Provided you're a good person and competent at something." **It may be their last annual raise, but the salary does not
drop.** Don: "Maybe there's a guy in a place where he doesn't
belong. Fine, he can be moved somewhere else. People move
around and sometimes mistakes are made. People are put in
the wrong position, and there's nothing wrong with taking
them out of that position and putting them in a different one."
**But if the person is unwilling to put out for CA the way CA is
willing to put out for him, he will be fired.** Charles: "You
bullshit, you die—simple as that." **And the person he reports
to will be the one to do it, because that person is responsible for
his work.** Don: "We fire enough people all the time, don't
worry about that. That's the thing I love about CA—you stay
only if you're really, really good here. There are no dead-
beats."

**When it is a case of someone not being able to do the work,
however, the stick that CA wields is loss of responsibility, perhaps with a couple of chances at other jobs.** Charles: "Just
don't pass around the turkeys." **But only up to a point.**
A middle manager: "This is not the kind of place where
you virtually have to murder someone to get fired. What I
really like about CA is it's almost like winning. It's like
only the best survive. What you have left is very brilliant
people."

While brilliant people are always in short supply, and even good people are not uniformly good at everything they do, most people are good at something. Arnie: "You can't have a company consisting only of brilliant people, but you can have a company that uses people brilliantly."

And the carrots? In corporate America these are typically divided into three separate bunches: (1) a framework of perks (tangible benefits at each salary level), (2) status symbols (usually intangible benefits), both of which are functions of (3) an unyielding salary schedule set by a chief of personnel.

Even if it wished to, CA is unable to emulate this neat, simple, traditional, and failing model. Lisa Mars: "At CA there is no minimum and maximum salary." Because where jobs are reinvented and reassigned across the entire company at least once a year—and sometimes far more often at the departmental level—job descriptions do not exist. Don: "It can happen anytime. A few years back it was in April, but more recently in October–November. People get moved around. People who are doing well move into other positions. Same for people who aren't." This means a stable organizational chart cannot exist. Don: "Shakes it up, keeps the adrenaline going." Without a stable chart, a salary scale cannot exist. Lisa: "There is no salary structure." In any practical sense a traditional compensation policy is thus impossible. Lisa: "Sometimes it happens that one person will earn more than the person he reports to."

Wait a minute. If a perk at what we'll call level-six marketing is a company car and stock options, what happens if the same manager is moved to level five in another part of the organization—say, sales? Does she lose her car and give up her options—

or the stock itself? (As we'll see, this hypothetical construct can't exist at CA anyway, because no one gets a car,* and the company is so flat that essentially there are just three levels: inner, middle, and outer.) Or say another manager's status symbol is a secretary to answer his phone? Paul: "I know for sure that if you call the executive vice president for North America at Colgate-Palmolive, where I used to work, there is absolutely no chance you could get to him on a phone call or that he would even call you back. Here it's a rare day when Arnie will say, 'Paul, can you call him back for me?' Arnie will do it himself. When a salesman needs an answer and they can't get to their divisional leaders, they call me. Outsiders are amazed that people call and I pick up the phone directly." **Or an office with a window?** Pete Schwartz: "What would I do with a window?" **What happens when responsibilities grow or shrink?**

The predictable. When the inflexible perks/status/salary grid is superimposed on a roiling, multidimensional organization whose only constancy is change, inevitably something has to give, usually with a resounding crack. Yet impracticality is not the reason CA has never attempted to solve this problem, because for CA, the problem itself does not exist.

Its employees' needs are not tied to those of the company peripherally, but intrinsically.

At most companies compensation is designed to superimpose the company's needs on those of its employees. This tactic evolves

---

*Outside the United States some employees do receive cars as part of their compensation package, but only because local business custom requires it.

from an awful dissonance economists normally take for granted: the aims of the corporation and those of its functionaries are forever doomed to remain in violent opposition. Historically this has always been the case—for a hundred years labor and management have literally spilled blood because of it. In theory the situation still exists, if only because the corporation represents the needs of its shareholders, not its employees.

Baldly stated, the needs of the shareholders are to employ the best people (among other assets) but always at the lowest cost. The needs of employees can be plotted as a function of both job security and pay, with some willing to sacrifice a bit more of the one for a bit less of the other. (See graphs 1a and 1b.) Yet there is another variable, conspicuous in most companies by its absence. Charles: "When you get a dedicated guy, pay him

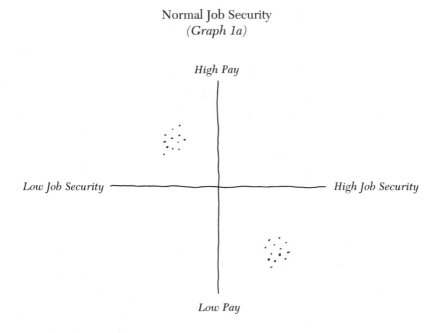

Normal Job Security
(Graph 1a)

High Pay

Low Job Security

High Job Security

Low Pay

twice as much, because you can eliminate three other people." **The never-asked question: what happens when higher pay for fewer individuals gets more work done than lower pay for more individuals?** Pete: "When I was at Xerox, the Latin American group was about an $800 million operation, probably similar to Computer Associates now, given some inflation. The financial organization was probably a hundred fifty to two hundred people. Here it's fifty." **Son of a gun. Are we saying that work can be so structured as to preclude low productivity by offering great incentives to those who work harder, better, faster, smarter?** Pete: "We have the right people. Some may be smarter, but the right people are better by necessity. More hardworking. When I bring somebody in, I'm not particularly hung up on technical or work experience. I'm looking for somebody who's hungry. I like people who are

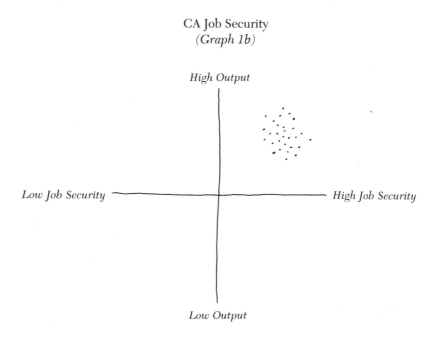

CA Job Security
(Graph 1b)

hungry and aggressive. That'll make up for a lot of shortcomings." Absolutely.

But immediately another problem raises its head: according to the spirit of the traditional workplace, if work is meant to pay well, then it is bound to be unsatisfying; if it is meant to produce satisfaction, it is bound to pay little. Most jobs are a compromise between these two variables. (See graphs 2a and 2b.) What happens when these supposedly antithetical elements aren't? CA has so arranged it, by a very simple device.

It doesn't hire—or quickly rids itself of—people who don't like to work. Pete: "My friends who are still at Xerox are making a lot less, but then they're working less too. Mostly they're just golfing, so they may be doing better on a per-hour basis.

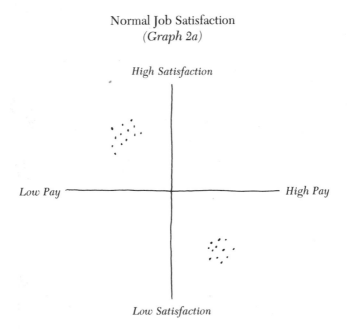

Normal Job Satisfaction
(Graph 2a)

107

But I enjoy hard work. I get bored on the weekends." **Simple: If your aims are not CA's, you just don't work here.** Pete: "The guys who are not hungry don't stay long. Even the guys who have gotten rich—Tony and Charles have gotten very rich— still are hungry enough to get their rocks off playing the game. They're still in here six days a week." **It follows that if your aims and CA's are the same (or at least congruent), then what is good for CA is good for you and what is good for you is good for CA.**

This calls for a second look at the object of all this carrot-and-stick waving. If our donkey likes to go to market, he will get there whether rewarded or threatened. Of course, this means he is not so much of a little ass at all but a partner or, with less legal baggage attached, an associate.

CA Job Satisfaction
(Graph 2b)

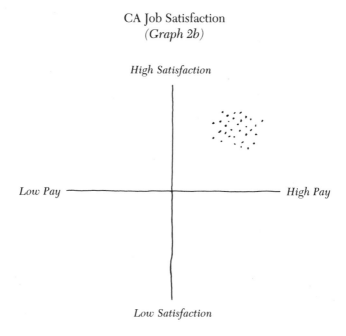

High Satisfaction

Low Pay ———————————————— *High Pay*

Low Satisfaction

Indeed, for a time Charles and some of CA's innermost circle seriously debated stripping away all titles and using only John Doe, Associate, or Jane Doe, Member. The idea was shelved, not least because it smacked of a pompous egalitarianism suggesting that everyone at CA is functionally equal. This is as clearly untrue as it is untenable in a company with close to eight thousand employees, some of whom earn twenty thousand dollars a year and some a hundred times that. But that CA even considered this kind of change demonstrates how deeply its corporate revolution goes. The notion is a contradiction in its own terms—it can't work. In avoiding hypocrisy, CA encouraged the only true equality—that of opportunity.

Rewarding the successful now became a problem so constructed that it had but one solution. Status symbols depend on a hierarchy, so they have neither place nor use. Perks, which tend to grow into an elaborate framework, must likewise be trashed. The reward for taking on more responsibility and succeeding with it?

Cash.

Not only does cash instantly signal reward, but the stuff is discrete: no one knows but the recipient and the person who has authorized the amount. This discretion permits employees to be rewarded according to their value to the company, not according to their placement in the hierarchy. As intriguing, since no one else knows how much you make, there is no reason to believe that one employee is intrinsically superior or better-favored than the next. At CA you may think you know who you're dealing with, but you can never be sure. So treat everyone with respect.

If this sounds egalitarian, it is. In fact, it brings to mind nothing less than a business parallel with the most radical rethinking of its time—and perhaps, still, of ours. What the French Revolution offered was a stripping away not of privilege but of *accumulated* privilege, *inherited* perks, status *entrenched* through nothing more than accidents of birth. Likewise, free of disembodied and irredeemable perks and status symbols, CA employees enjoy an equality of opportunity—the opportunity to succeed—that is so pure as to be stirring. But the really stirring part is not the benefit to its employees, but what it does to CA as a company.

VI. Nickels and Dimes

Following CA's acquisition of Uccel, Sanjay Kumar began traveling regularly from Dallas to Long Island. Sanjay: "I came to Garden City a few times after that, and it was funny because the very first time I came, I spoke to Charles on the phone and he gave me directions: 'Stay at the Garden City Hotel. Here's how you get there. Garden City Hotel. Stay there. Only the Garden City Hotel. That's where you stay." I said OK. Really nice hotel, gorgeous building. And then the merger between the two companies was complete—there had been a waiting period—and suddenly I was booked into the Island Inn, from a hundred-eighty-dollar hotel to an eighty-dollar hotel. Meanwhile, in Dallas I was having to defend CA. We'd have corporate recruiters flying in to raid the company. At least fifteen guys came to see me in Dallas, including two guys that came in on their corporate jet. A lot of people didn't like CA. And one of the things they said was it was cheap. 'CA is cheap, and we're going to have another layoff. They're going to screw us.' Which, of course, CA didn't, because when we say there's only going to be one cut in an acquisition, that's it. There's not going to be another one. And I had to convince my guys at what had been Uccel that CA didn't do that. But it was harder to convince them CA wasn't cheap after they moved me from the Garden City Hotel to the Island Inn. And it was a very frustrating, very physically taxing time. Every Thursday I was in Garden City, so I'd take the Wednesday night flight, the last flight up, and I'd land at twelve-thirty in

111

the morning, drive out here. The plane was often late. I would get to the Island Inn, which nowadays has been fixed up, but it used to be a real dump, and it would be two o'clock in the morning. I'd sleep until seven, meet with Russ and Charles all day long, and take a seven o'clock flight back home to Dallas." **Which is how he learned just how unique CA's cost culture is.** Sanjay: "And one night I came to the Island Inn—Not the nicest place, but it was OK. I mean, you sleep there for five hours, big deal. And the biggest insult was being bumped from the Island Inn because they were full. And being bumped, if you had a guaranteed reservation, they owe you a room somewhere else, right? They put me in the Coliseum Motor Inn. This is a place where teenagers rented rooms by the hour. So we are talking about kids walking in and out of this place all night long, cars in and out of the parking lot. And I lay there and thought, *There is one consolation in all of this. They are no longer treating me like someone who Charles felt should be put up at an expensive hotel.* They were treating me like CA." **It is uniquely cheap.**

This is not to say that CA employees don't get perks. Beyond the usual medical plan and stock options, there is a fully equipped and staffed health club open twenty-four hours a day; the cafeteria is subsidized; the cost of academic courses is reimbursed 100 percent; and breakfast is laid on five days a week. But these are not the products of Santa's corporate workshop. There is a hardheadedness behind each decision.

The health club? Right or wrong, Charles Wang happens to believe healthy bodies are good for healthy minds. The cafeteria? Invariably CA offices are sited on the periphery of large cities, usually closer to airports than any decent place to eat. This

not only cuts down on the time and expense of getting to and from airports, but where weeds are high real estate prices aren't. Of course, eating in-house encourages people to work through lunch. And yes, academic courses are paid for, but only if "the course is degree and job related and has as its purpose the enhancement of your skills in your existing position at CA." And if you get a B grade or better. And if you keep working for CA. So don't expect to sleep through an M.A. in basket-weaving and then quit the company. The idea, according to a company flyer, is "to make [employees] even greater assets to the company's growth and expansion."

That's why CA's new headquarters building at Islandia, New York—farther from New York City than the old site but within spitting distance of Long Island–MacArthur, one of the best-connected small airports in the country—has a fully staffed child-care center. CA's position on kids is unknown, but its position on getting the most out of their parents is clear.

Breakfast? The company's logo should be a jelly donut. Breakfast *is* CA. When Charles began the company, he'd bring in donuts every morning for his staff. Three employees, three donuts. Four employees, four donuts. This isn't uncommon in small businesses, but Charles didn't quit. As the company grew, Charles continued to bring in the donuts, as well as—depending on the day of the week—bagels, muffins, Danish pastries, buttered rolls, and fresh fruit. When someone noticed that Charles was bringing in several hundred donuts every morning, the job was taken away—but not the donuts. These remained. A perk, like a paycheck, doesn't get reduced or taken away, unless you're fired.

Once the idiosyncratic habit of an entrepreneur making up for low salaries by bringing his employees breakfast out of his own pocket, the practice now costs the company over $1 million a year in donuts and—because half CA's revenues are earned abroad—in croissants, churros, brötchen, pitas, pãozinhos, and scones. Though it's possible to argue that breakfast in the office encourages people to get to work early, the impetus probably comes from somewhere else. When the air-conditioning broke down at 711 Stewart Avenue during a Long Island heat wave, a man in shirtsleeves appeared in the corridors at CA headquarters wheeling around the kind of ice cream cart likely to be found in any municipal park. To this day it is not known whether any of the CA staff who were meeting with a group of clients in a conference room bothered to tell their rather stiff guests that the man with the ice cream cart was Charles B. Wang, who had earlier begged off from attending the meeting because "something hot came up."

What sets these perks apart is neither their hardheadedness nor their quality, which to one extent or another are nothing new, but their absolute parity. They are uncompromisingly egalitarian. The donuts are no sweeter for CA's inner circle than for the blue-collar crew in the mailroom.

This egalitarian strain applies to more than donuts. Before CA's recent move to new corporate headquarters, Tony's office was smaller than those of dozens of people reporting to him, smaller even than managers two or three levels down. Tony: "In most companies it's different. Let's say a manager is paid more than the troops, but instead of a large office, he sits in the same type of cubicle as the troops. The troops don't see any incentive. They don't know the salaries of the managers. All they see are people like themselves working much harder with the same apparent incentives. There are people who need to see the tangible rewards in the perks. For us it's in the job itself and in the pay, straight pay." But at least he has a window. Most of the people mentioned in this book don't. And not one of them, including Charles, has a gatekeeping secretary to keep people away or create even as much as the appearance of a barrier. Judy Cedeno, who assists Charles, has her own office down the hall. Tony: "Anyone walks into Charles' office or into mine. From Arnie to messengers with problems. Secretaries don't front offices. There are no barriers."

In fact, at CA's new, sleekly functional world headquarters building in Islandia, New York, there are barely any walls at all. Designed around an atrium, the building provides an integrated work environment for CA personnel previously at four separate locations in Garden City, thirty miles west. The architecture is utilitarian, which is pretty much what anyone might expect from the kind of company that has outgrown three other corporate headquarters in sixteen years, but what surprises visitors who know CA is something else: it looks good.

The old Garden City offices seemed to reflect a purposeful vision of CA as a company that cared more about the bottom line than the top floor. These former offices were furnished with a ragtag collection of often glaringly mismatched desks and chairs; the odd set that looked good also managed to look out of place, like the yards-long teak boardroom table and matching chairs acquired from a company CA had taken over. Arnie: "Every time we made an acquisition we upgraded our furniture." Another exception was Tony's office, which had the understated elegance of a London club. Tony: "This furniture is all mine—I brought it with me. When I came on, Charles' memo to the staff welcoming me said, 'The best thing about Tony is he's bringing his own furniture.' He was afraid others would want to upgrade if they thought CA was paying for it."

During the moving-in period, visitors were shocked at the high quality of the furnishings being unloaded at Islandia. Even Guy Porre, managing director of CA-France from its inception, was surprised. Guy: "It was so much better than I had ever seen at CA, in the United States or France or anywhere. Whole suites of exceptional things. Then I saw a desk I thought I recognized. Yes, it was from Princeton, from what had once been ADR. It dawned on me that all of this had come from failed companies, companies that had spent grandly on decor but not enough on products, on technology, on marketing. The symbolism was compelling." Like the fully equipped television studio that CA had inherited in the assets of a company it had acquired and had put to use to produce all its own training films in-house, six floors of furniture is now being put to use at Islandia in a kind of cleverly marshaled trompe l'oeil. Some of this stuff had been mothballed for years; in the case of equipment from ADR, since 1988. George C. Tatter, vice president: "Ordinarily the ADR furniture would have been removed and sold, and the offices broken down and used less opulently by CA. But we had the idea we were going to sell the whole building, and executive offices like that are a plus to companies that aren't like CA. Then the real estate market dropped. So it all just sat there, shrink-wrapped. No one ever went in there."

Should this prove fascinating to future archaeologists digging into the culture of *Homo industrus americanus*, this generation's scholars don't even have to dig. In Dallas the writing was literally on the wall. After CA bought Uccel in 1987, all work on the acquired company's new headquarters building was reconsidered from the CA point of view. In the lobby the marble that covered the floor and was supposed to run up the walls was simply canceled in midrun. It's hard to imagine a more graphic illustration of the distinction between Uccel's Athens and CA's Sparta. Tony: "After we acquired Uccel, we scaled down the elegance in the new building Uccel was going to move into the following year. In the lobby, where we stopped the marble halfway up the wall, someone had drawn an arrow and a sign that said 'CA acquires Uccel.' " There was something else noticeably different about the building Uccel designed. CA decided not to bother finishing it. Arnie: "When we acquired Uccel, they had committed to very luxurious offices, a whole tower, nineteen stories. It was under construction when we acquired the company. The real estate market had just died. Well, they hadn't yet put up the ceilings. We saved six hundred thousand dollars by not putting up ceilings. On the one hand, you had this luxurious tower, and on the other you could look up and there were all the wires and vents because there were no ceilings."

While CA parking lots claim more than their normal share of Mercedes and BMWs, the elegance stays outdoors; inside, the sense of lean and mean borders on the driven. When a roll of stamps was burgled out of Arnie's desk, Tony had a video camera installed in one of the cartons stacked shoulder-high around Arnie's office. The thinking was that the culprit, possibly someone on the night staff—security, maintenance, data center, support—would strike again. In any other company the solution would be simpler: lock your door, lock your desk, don't leave valuables in the office. But at CA, where trust is next to godliness, petty theft has all the inconsequentiality of murder one.

End of story? Only the beginning. Remember the game in which you're given a drawing and asked, "What's wrong with this picture?" and someone's earlobe has been drawn upside down? Look again, then, at Arnie's office, and ask yourself what kind of nearly $2 billion corporation is it where a senior manager has an office full of cartons? Arnie: "Everything's in cartons. These are cartons from three years ago when we bought ADR in Princeton, and then after I handled that, I came up here. I don't even know what's in them anymore. Someday I'll get to them, but meanwhile I tell guests they're not just cartons, they're *designer* cartons. These are the same people I always make it a point to walk past Charles' office so I can point out his plywood desk and tell them, 'You see, *all* the money goes into the software.' " Now ask yourself what Arnie Mazur was doing with twenty bucks' worth of stamps in his desk drawer? Doesn't CA have a mailroom? It does, but only for CA mail.

All of us have sent personal letters on the company tab, especially those ubiquitous credit card bills we keep forgetting to pay at home. For most, this is not much of an ethical dilemma. To those at the bottom of the organizational totem pole, it's something you can get the company to pay for that no one will miss, so why not? At the top it's a single stamp that compares rather anemically to yesterday's two-hundred-dollar lunch. After all, what's twenty-nine cents to GE, Time Inc., Prudential Life, Beatrice Foods, or any local Ford dealership? Mike Picker: "I just hate it when people sit around talking on the phone when they're supposed to be working. I just hate it. It's not right." What it is to CA is a betrayal of basic trust.

Besides, this is a company where they physically lock up the seven-and-a-half-cent ballpoints nobody wants to use, much less take home; where paper clips are a line item in someone's budget; where you can get a computer, even two or three if you need them, but don't expect to find a mine of Post-it notes to decorate the screens. To say that CA is careful about its money is to say that professional basketball players are above average in height.

Unconvinced? This is a place where the Christmas season initiates extra vigilance on the supply of cellophane tape. Judy Holt, administrative assistant: "You know, for wrapping presents? It can just all disappear." Of course, not a lot of people have a chance to play with the office supplies, which makes the vigilance easier. CA's entire finance department, fifty people, has one secretary. Pete: "People type. People answer their own phone. Nothing wrong with that."

If for no other reason, CA may become famous in the annals of American business for its awe-inspiring ability to squeeze a nickel until it looks, acts, and smells like twelve bucks. Tony: "We hate to waste money, and it's so easy to waste. On a public offering we had to print prospectuses. Alex. Brown & Sons were doing it, and they said we'd need thirty thousand copies. I knew how many it took. I was a Wall Street lawyer. Why do you need thirty thousand? You're lucky if you need five thousand. It's because that's the norm for them, thirty thousand. After a few phone calls the number came down to ten thousand—and I'm sure there are copies lying around in someone's closet gathering dust. Was it the end of the world? No. It was another five thousand copies of an offering statement. So maybe people shouldn't question that. I remember the man from Alex. Brown saying, 'Five thousand?' But then again, most companies don't provide breakfast for every employee. We can do that *because* we're cheap. So we can afford to." **When Lynn Weitzner arrived on the job in 1989 as CA purchasing manager responsible for office supplies, the cost for office necessities was forty-three dollars per employee. The next year she got it down to twenty-seven. For 1991 she figures she will have hit twenty to twenty-one. Adjusted for inflation, that's a real reduction of about 70 percent over three years.** Lynn: "I also clip grocery coupons at home. I can't stand paying more money than I should. Nobody is driving me to get these prices lower. It's in my nature—as well as CA's." **But maybe this is just penny-wise.** Jay: "Spartan is reflected in the bottom line, though the cost culture isn't as pervasive at the lower levels as it used to be. It's just harder to do that as you get larger and keep all the parts thinking about it, especially when you have a lot of people here that come from acquired companies like Uccel and Cullinet, where there wasn't that culture, where the heroes were the guys who spent the most as opposed to the guys who got the most for least." **And pound-foolish.** Jay: "Tony uses me as a guy who makes sure there isn't money wasted here. I simply fight for every right and proper use of the nickels and dimes and dollars and hundreds of millions of dollars that CA spends. What's in my heart is I view myself as a protector of CA assets and I take corporate and personal pride when I have struck the best deal this company could possibly have gotten." **Don't kid yourself.** Denise Carr, controller, CA United Kingdom: "When I make a two-and-a-half million-pound purchase, I always feel, 'Why didn't I get it for two million?' " **But that would mean cost cutting as a value would be built in as an integral part of business culture.** David J. Wardle, president of CA's Asia-Pacific Group: "Most companies wouldn't think of buying things the way CA does. When our purchasing people look at a piece of computer equipment that costs sixty-five-thousand dollars new and fifteen thousand used, the miracle is not that they'll take the lower cost item—maybe they will and maybe they won't. There are trade-offs either way. The miracle is that at CA we look. We check. We treat cost-cutting seriously." **For American business, cost cutting isn't built in—it's built out.** Mike: "When I look at the budget I control, it's about fifty million dollars, so I try to teach my people the art of negotiating. Our people have to negotiate. We go to places and ask for quotes. Many companies do a little of that, but they just take the lowest price. We have a little formula here that's different. We use it to arrive at a price, then we go back to the vendor and say, 'If you want this job, this is our approved quote.' Our vendor may think that someone came in lower and that's why he's got to meet that price, but actually that's just our own little formula. When you're talking a certain percent of hundreds of millions of dollars, you're talking about saving a big amount of money." **How can we logically expect frugality to be a value in a business environment in which the quality of a department or an individual is judged not on how much is saved, but on how much is spent?** Mike: "Well, you might say to yourself, 'Hey, some of these items are only two hundred dollars on the purchase order so big deal, what's twenty dollars? But it's ten dollars here and twenty there. I tell them to look at it as if it's their own money, because in a lot of places outside of CA, it's 'So what, it's the company's money,' and they sign the purchase order because who needs the aggravation of another phone call? But that's not what we teach. We teach it is your own money. If you want the right to spend it, it is yours."

In American companies aggressive people go into sales. They rarely go into quality control, seldom go into research and development, never go into purchasing—there's no glory in it.

Outside of CA, certainly not even the most aggressive purchasing manager—not even a dementedly aggressive one—will look seriously at used furniture. A purchasing manager: "Sure we acquire chairs when we acquire companies, but we buy chairs too, now and then: fifty-nine ninety-five." And then reject it as too expensive. The purchasing manager: "Our furniture, when we buy it, is actually cheaper than used. I've bumped into that. Because used furniture is typically very high-quality furniture. People who deal in used furniture don't sell junk." Because there's even cheaper stuff out there. The purchasing manager: "And we buy it! I mean, if you buy a five-thousand-dollar chair and you get it used, five hundred bucks may be great—but we probably only pay one hundred, so it doesn't make sense for us." And it's even cheaper. The purchasing manager: "Functional is the issue at CA, not pretty. I mean obviously." Because in your nice, normal, well-run American company, there's no glamour in saving money. "Memo to: ALL CA EMPLOYEES. Re: AIRBORNE PROCEDURES. In those offices that do not have mailrooms and for those people who put your Airbornes directly into the Airborne Drop Box, you must declare a weight. ALL packages, including Letter Express Paks, must have a weight written on the airbill. If you are not exactly sure of the weight, please give your best estimate—but put *something*. Any Airborne package that does not have a weight specified on the airbill will automatically be charged the 5 lb. average rate of $13.29; i.e., a Letter Express Pak with a declared weight of 1 pound would cost CA $6.79. The same package without a declared weight would cost CA $13.29. Since CA is trying, as always, to cut unnecessary expenditures, it is very important to avoid incurring this type of charge. Also, please be sure to combine all Airborne packages being sent to the same CA office address, i.e., sixteen packages all being sent from Long Island to the Irving [Texas] office individually would cost $7.32 each, $117.12 total. Those 16 packages combined into one package only costs $25.00. If those 16 packages are not combined, it costs CA an additional $92.12." **That's because even at the best-run companies no one seems to have figured out that the more money you save the more you have.** "From: TONY McALEAR. Re: ELECTRICAL COSTS FOR EQUIPMENT USAGE. It has been brought to my attention that many people feel they should be leaving their PCs powered on while they are not in use. This is not the case. Turning off your PC in no way causes any problem in the functioning of the unit, in fact turning off the unit can save a large amount of money. It costs approximately 12.5 cents per hour to run 1 PC. There are 168 hours in one week. This means that there are 128 non-working hours per PC. The cost for one PC left on is $16 per week or $830 per year. There are 250 PCs in the Westwood locations. If everyone left their PC on all of the time, the cost would be $207,000 per year. There are 100 DEC terminals in the Westwood area at a cost of $30,000 per year for off-hours electrical usage. After doing some off-hours checking I noted almost all of the IBM and DEC terminals were left on and about 50 percent of the PCs were left running. Based on these observations we are wasting $185,000 per year in unnecessary electrical charges. Please turn off all equipment that is not being used both during and outside of regular working hours. Your cooperation will be greatly appreciated. Thank you." **This is why CA is able to invest 13** percent of revenues on research and development, higher than the norm for established technology companies, including Microsoft, and far higher than IBM's anorexic 9.5 percent. "To: ALL CA EMPLOYEES. From: DON OSLEY. Re: ELECTRICITY CONSERVATION. Recently Tony McAlear, the Westwood PC tech, issued a note regarding the electricity consumption of idle terminals/PCs. As mentioned in the note, quite a lot of money can be saved by turning off equipment when you leave for the evening/weekend. While electricity costs will vary from location to location, if everyone were to turn off their equipment when leaving the office each day, I estimate the yearly saving could exceed $1,000,000 in electricity costs. Please take the time to read Tony's note and please cooperate by turning off all equipment (PCs, printers, modems and terminals) when not in use."

A million here, a million there is why CA has been able continually to acquire companies that have spent their way to oblivion. "To: ALL CA EMPLOYEES U.S. ONLY. From: LYNN WEITZNER. Re: SPECIAL AIRBORNE PRICING. EFFECTIVE IMMEDIATELY, CA has arranged a special discounted OVERNIGHT rate with Airborne for 0–5 lb. packages that require delivery prior to 3:00 P.M. within the continental United States. This represents a savings of almost 50 percent compared to next morning delivery! Please note that in the past all overnight packages were sent at a substantially higher rate for Express Delivery (P1) which guarantees delivery prior to 12:00 P.M. the next business day. In most instances the three hour difference should have little effect. Therefore, this new service should be our standard overnight service and we should only use the P1 in rare circumstances. Please contact me directly if you have any questions. Based on our $ volume, CA can save almost $200,000 a year with this new service." And that is why people at CA understand that saving money means more money to spend on what's really necessary, like superhigh salaries, like new technology, like not being out of a job because your bosses are spending like wildfire on themselves and starving the company.

This issue of corporate responsibility, to employees as well as shareholders, is one that corporate America will continue to ignore at its own risk. Nothing better spells out this message than a relatively insignificant event that occurred on November 5, 1991, as CA's $282 million acquisition of Pansophic Software took effect.

Charles was at Pansophic's headquarters in Lisle, Illinois, directing the transition. Only shortly before, CA had acquired On-Line Software at a price of $90 million. These two major and some minor acquisitions during the same period meant significant restructuring at CA, heavy but careful cuts of personnel at the acquired companies (50 percent of personnel is normally let go, more than half of these in the bloated executive layers), and a melding of the development, support, marketing, and sales divisions of the acquired companies into CA. In a matter of days CA went through a careful process of integration that saw its payroll rise from seven thousand to close to eight thousand employees.

That the chairman of a company reaching toward the $2 billion revenue mark found the time to think of how CA was spending its money with regard to these new employees is something in and of itself. "To: ALL NEW CA EMPLOYEES. From: CHARLES B. WANG. One would think that there are more important things to which I should pay attention, but sometimes I find that 'insignificant details' include the invisible items that make our workday more pleasant for everybody. Hopefully the following items qualify: (a) Breakfast donuts, croissants, etc. will be distributed to the various coffee stations . . . ; (b) The former 'executive' parking area at Lisle will now be made available to persons who can benefit from the convenience (i.e., pregnant or ill persons). For more information please contact Margie Steck (6240) to arrange for that convenient parking spot during your period of need; (c) Lunch today at Lisle will be offered at half the normal price. Enjoy!" That Charles Wang actually did something—on the spot making the delicate but positive changes that allow CA's carefully saved nickels and dimes to benefit those on whom the company depends—is without parallel in American corporate management. "(d) The normal business hours for Lisle and other Chicago area offices [formerly 8:30 A.M. to 5:00 P.M.] will be 9:00 A.M. to 5:00 P.M." Anyone for a donut?

Part Three:

Culture

I. Work

When we speak of national or corporate culture, we are speaking of the evidence of character, because underlying all culture is character. In the case of corporate culture, it is the skeletal structure to which the muscle and sinew of business is attached. Without character, what we call business culture is little more than business personality—the smile, not the attitude; the decision, not the values that made it inevitable. So without closely examining the elements of underlying character, to look at CA as an exemplary twenty-first-century business culture is as delusive and futile as looking at Japanese business culture in order to identify elements of its personality and then putting them on like makeup or a hat.

Yes, Japanese success may be predicated on (among other things) a remarkable ability to design products consumers want and the parallel ability to organize a work force and suppliers who produce those items and whose loyalty to the company is extreme by any standard. But can these elements be successfully emulated? Will General Motors' Saturn Division, to take the nineties' best-advertised example, succeed in its costly attempt to capture a chunk of the U.S. car market by duplicating these two personality traits of Japanese corporate culture?

Prophecy is not yet an exact science, but asking the right questions does suggest some answers.

Are Japanese car companies successful because they put design first? Or do they put design first because of a thousand-year tradition of building even the most mundane objects so that they are aesthetically correct, human in feel and scale, and thus intrinsically desirable?

If Japanese companies inspire employee loyalty through cradle-to-grave security, then how is it English socialism inspired little more than high absenteeism and low productivity while Marxist-Leninism brought forth only that permanent state of organized fraud in which, according to the classic Russian formula, "We pretend to work and they pretend to pay us"?

Clearly Japanese success in creating an almost feudal sense of loyalty has more to do with the fact that Japanese society was so recently feudal itself. Dressing up Detroit assembly-line workers in Japanese-style Saturn uniforms and moving them south to do Japanese calisthenics every morning is about as sensible as trying to turn them into Cordon Bleu chefs by teaching them French and pelting them with goose livers. *Non, monsieur,* goose livers maketh not the man, and copying the corporate tics and tricks of CA, 3M, Swissair, or any other company is not going to create the same kind of success stories.

If we are to learn anything at all, what we have to get right is an understanding of the underlying values, which in the case of CA we have not yet done. We've looked only at the mechanics. These may reflect the values but do not illuminate them.

According to the twentieth-century business creed, management is the preeminent function in business and what used to be called labor (current euphemisms are *work force, employees, personnel*) is a kind of passive tail wagged by a highly skilled

130

dog. In direct contrast to this common wisdom, CA tends to look at management from the point of view of that most basic unit of production, the garden-variety human being, for whom the primary engine of industry is a concept both elementary and largely misunderstood. It is called work.

Of course, not all work is the same, not even in concept. At CA it is so different from work as we have come to accept it that it must ultimately be reclassified as something else, something that seems to be the same but isn't, much in the way some newly discovered form of sea life may look, swim, and smell like a fish but on close inspection turns out to be a genus heretofore unknown. Self-determined, measurable, and at the same time limitless, CA work is an amorphous endeavor whose success or failure may ultimately be gauged at the bottom line but, at the very same time, must always be judged against the relative success of the work of others, just as an individual baseball player's value is sometimes determined on such things as runs batted in but is always judged against the relative success of other players on the same team. Regardless of how it is measured, the value of the work of individuals is so important to CA that in sum it defies and ignores the twentieth-century credo that companies succeed or fail only because of decisions made in the penthouse. CA's culture of work—on the shop floor and everywhere else—is what makes CA work.

Such a direct cause-and-effect mechanism obviously puts some pressure on the meaning of the word as we know it. In fact, it just about transmogrifies it.

> work *n* (werk): (1) a measurable unit of effort over time, as judged against that of others; (2) the same, but which may only be accomplished with the very

same others; (3) the profitable and/or well-rewarded process of same; (4) the endless, limitless, or unbounded process of same; (5) contractual and ethical selflessness. [*See also* labor (rental of body or mind absent satisfaction, sense, or goal); job (rental of body or mind for effort so circumscribed its only reward is material).]

II. Measurable

Though we've looked at ranking from the point of view of management, the perspective changes when we look at it through the eyes of the managed. To get the most or best work done, management must be in a position to know which employee contributes the most. But since really valuable work is performed in a uniquely changing universe of many variables, it is not possible to judge it on a units-per-hour basis, which, at this stage of industrial history, is (or will soon be) intrinsically limited to the repetitive low-value work of the machine. Even when two people produce in parallel—say, when two salesmen are working the same size territory—the territories are different. Worse, measurement becomes all the more difficult when we attempt to judge the work that goes into part of a process, such as the value of publicity generated by a public relations officer: maybe the product is a dud, but she's done wonders with it; maybe she's a dud, but the product makes her look good. That is why CA's method of judging the value of work is to ascertain the comparative value of individuals, one against the next. Yet here we immediately run into a paradox.

The work is individual, but to be effective, it must be performed in concert with the work of others, the same others against whom the individual is rated and ranked. Thus the first requirement bumps into and is modified by the second: no matter how good you are, you can't do it alone. In fact, doing it alone means not really doing it, so from the individual's point of view, simple

133

competitiveness is therefore not only not feasible but destructive. For example, the programmer whose brilliance is untempered by regard for the contributions and needs of others is essentially drawing attention only to his own accomplishments, however awesome they may be, by destroying the accomplishments of others. Reuven: "A few people like this can disturb the ability of others to get a job done. There was one group I had, about forty-eight people, that for many years was regarded as the worst in the company. It turned out that most of the people were very good, but they were all working in the shadow of these other people, who insisted that things had to be done their way. So I let four people go, four out of forty-eight working on a series of interrelated products, and suddenly we had a change. It's now definitely one of the best places to work in the company, and they've developed new products that have had a tremendous success in the market. Four people."

III. With Others

In theory, by working in combination with others we are able to increase the value of our work. But not always. Though two people rowing may be expert, muscular, and dedicated individuals, if they don't row in harmony and in the same direction, they are not likely to get where they want to go, not quickly anyhow. In fact, one rower in a darting scull can beat a thousand in a megahull when five hundred are rowing one way and five hundred more are efficiently spinning the whole thing around by rowing the other.

In the western tradition the originators of cooperative rowing were the Greeks, stubborn individualists who nevertheless banded together voluntarily from time to time for some great outing, like the sack of Troy. But as much as they loved a good cooperative pillage, the Greeks we read about in *The Iliad* were unreflective egoists who constantly questioned the wisdom and authority of their leaders, especially when things did not look too good in the short term. They were simply unable to trust anyone else's vision of victory just around the corner. This failing turned out to be terrific for Homer, who literally dined out on his stories, and good for us as well because these squabbles begat the concept of differences of opinion peacefully settled, which was to become a basic tenet of democracy. Still, it made for a hellish way to try to run a ship. Half the crew might be rowing while the other half sat around discussing it. Anarchy—not any lack of nautical skill—is why the Greeks were famously poor seamen, who consequently always felt most comfortable within sight of land, which meant being so close to the rocks that the entire *Odyssey* has been aptly described as one long shipwreck interrupted by brief periods at sea.

Solving the problem called for strong central management, practically a Roman invention. By instituting compulsion (slavery) and fear (the lash), Roman galleys were able to travel fast and far enough to build and maintain a great empire. Now everyone was pulling in the same direction, but a crew of beaten galley slaves was not real motivated. The word *mutiny* still reeks of the sea.

Command management has been with us a long time—and is still practicable, especially where the work to be done is essentially the work of human machines. But when the work demands creativity and initiative, compulsion and fear are the wrong way to get it done.

As we move from the twentieth century into a future in which the work of human machines will more and more be done by real machines, human work will by definition become creative (at least in the sense that rote responses will not suffice), incentive driven (there's a payoff for doing more), and self-motivated (*you* define what more is). As a bare minimum for participation, a kind of Greco-Roman compromise takes hold: while retaining its independence, so that its members may leave at any time, the crew is encouraged for the common good to seek ways to get the ship moving efficiently, though the ultimate decision always rests with the captain. Charles: "The reasoning is group reasoning, but the decision making is singular. There are some people who can't stand the first part of that. They want to make all the decisions in their department on their own, without any connection to whatever else is going on. And there are people who don't like it when the decision is made and it's not theirs. Either way, I say, 'Oh, you're good, you can get a job anywhere. Why don't you? You'd be happier somewhere else.' " **In what we're virtually compelled to call one stroke, this replaces management (the mentality of command: any private interests you may have, take care of after five o'-clock) with leadership (getting the most out of others voluntarily: keep your private interests, but frame them within a commonality of interest).**

So that yours and theirs are not mutually exclusive. Mike: "Everything we do here is as a team—the 'I's leave. They have to leave. Because their sense of survival is personal, it's not corporate, not communal. There are a couple of 'I's in my organization right now that I'm trying to show the way, but right now it's 'I, I, I, I, I.' You know, as in 'I do everything on my own,' but that's not what we do. We do it together. The success is not part of *I*, it's part of *we*." **The overlap between yours and theirs has a name: it's called *ours*.** *New York Times* advertisement, November 18, 1990: "HOW DO YOU BECOME THE LEADING PLAYER IN SOFTWARE? BY RECRUITING THE BEST TEAM. Computer Associates is the world's leading independent developer and supplier of computer software. And we've reached the top by putting together the brightest, most enthusiastic team in the business. . . . We are seeking the following professionals:

• Programmers with a PC background [list of technical requirements]. You must enjoy working with people.

• Programmers with a VAX background [tech requirements]. You must enjoy working with people.

• Programmers with an MVS or VSE Systems background

[tech requirements]. You must enjoy working with people. . . ."

And this principle leads directly to another: ego is not a necessary coefficient of talent. Mike: "When we acquired Uccel, it came down to the point where a lot of work had to be done in an extremely short time and it was going to be late. So we had someone go down to the airport and pick the stuff up off the plane from Dallas and bring it back to Garden City here at ten at night. It had to go out the next morning. So what we did was informally—without a memo, without anything—everybody, every manager, was asked to see some of their people. And I tell you, eighty or ninety percent of the people who were then at CA headquarters, including Tony, including presidents of divisions, came in to stuff envelopes and get that thing out. We had a couple of hundred people working, which means an enormous return-to-work rate at ten o'clock at night, and there was no memo, there was nothing saying you'd get paid overtime or what would happen. So you had people staying until three A.M. and later, even into the next day. That shows what kind of people we have. Nobody said you have to come. We just put out a little informal whisper that said, 'Hey, we could use some help,' and all these people showed up stuffing envelopes—not the most exciting way to spend a weeknight—and most of them showed up for work the next day."

So the single most significant factor in the ranking of managers at CA takes into account how much work they can get out of others: work at CA means getting others to work as hard as you do. Mike: "When I worked for a Big Eight accounting firm, it was 'Hey, fill out my time/expense report and bill back to

the customer for the time.' Routine. It not only wasn't team spirit, it was 'Who cares?' That's so far from CA it's hard to believe both are business. OK, obviously the CA person has to have something deep inside to get down to it the way we do it, but this work culture helps to bring it out of you if you do have it. I'd say nine out of ten people here will say they enjoy it and they are comfortable with the atmosphere, which is one reason we're able to get more work out of the people."
But it applies only if they can talk to you about it, and you can talk to them. Mike: "They say I'm able to get a lot of work out of people, but what it means is, with good people you just have to learn how to talk to them as people, not just workers on an org chart. They have to know that I'll support them if they screw up, which is oddly even more important than congratulating them when they do well, because when they do well, they know it, but when they screw up, it's awful when they don't know it. You're just looking for a repeat of the same problem, and it's painful for them and embarrassing. They know that when it comes up at my level, I'll say I screwed up, not them, that I won't say, 'Hey, it wasn't me,' but that I'll come to them later and we'll talk about it and figure out what went wrong. Look, there are maybe fifty jobs going on here at any one time, and I can't get involved in all of them. Sure, if someone messes up, I can easily go and say, 'I didn't do it,' and just sit there, but I won't do that because it doesn't make anything better. It just sticks blame on someone, so that I'd be saying 'You're bad,' instead of 'What you did was bad—now let's fix it, learn from it.' So when I take the blame on myself—everyone here has heard me say I blew it and it's my fault—everyone probably knows it's not my fault, and that person specifically knows I stood up for him and went the extra mile. It wasn't always that way around here,

but now when you talk to other groups in the company, they'll say, 'Hey, we have some confidence in that group,' whereas maybe four or five years ago they couldn't have said that. Which, when you think of it, is almost a joke, because before I came to CA the most I ever managed was eight people on an audit. What happened wasn't that I got shot through with truth serum; what happened was I learned. I learned by talking to people and listening. One of the things I was surprised about was how people get upset about things on and even off the job that I can fix. Like, there are many people within my group and within other groups who I do their financial statements for. I help them on their household budgets. I had a person here that was six or seven thousand dollars in debt, and I helped her figure out a way to deal with it. Personal stuff, yes, but I can help them because I have that background. What happens is that in time that person builds up confidence in me and says, 'Hey, he didn't have to do that. Maybe I can make mistakes, stretch myself, because he looks at me like a human being,' and 'Then, if I can make mistakes, so can he.' So everyone gets the idea that we're all allowed to give our opinion and everything is always fixable. So there's room for people who can learn and grow, and the worst thing that can happen, the worst punishment, is we might close the door and sit down and say, 'OK, you did that wrong, let's redo it. And there's no reason to get strained out or upset. The idea is to learn how to do it, and that's always learnable, because if I could learn, then everybody can. Hey, I'm an accountant. I'm not supposed to be able to do this, but I learned and you can too.' " **This calls for total, immediate, and effortless access up and down the line.** Roger Hipwell, U.K. sales manager: "Some companies have doors with names on them, some companies have doors with names in pencil, some with no names. CA doesn't have any doors." **Without exception.**

140

Look at every billion-dollar company in America—hell, in the solar system—and you will not find one in which a Pete Schwartz, as director of finance, happily takes a call from a Clay Chin, in the warehouse, who has just sold a surplus couch to an employee for twenty-five dollars and doesn't know what to do with the cash. Pete asks Clay to bring it to him; he'll deposit it himself.

Under such intimate conditions, which must be downright intimidating to those who are paid well not to know what is going on, no manager can detach himself from the blame that would in any other company stick to those he manages. That is precisely why CA people are ranked according to how well they can choose others, both initially and as part of an ongoing process of picking the best. Don: "In an acquisition we're looking for the best people to remain with us. We have to let some go, that's understood. The question becomes, 'What's the qualification for being picked to remain with CA?' " But the choice is based neither primarily nor necessarily on technical skills, résumé, or education. Don: "I just came back from Chicago, where we interviewed all the people from a new acquisition, and you see person after person. What it comes down to is attitude. There are people with a positive attitude and people with a negative attitude. With the odd exception—because they're nervous or you're not reading them right—you can tell from the moment they walk in. Attitude." Because in a company that is always doing something new, having done something well before is an advantage of quickly diminishing returns. Bob Toth: "I'm a C.P.A. by trade, so when I came here to be interviewed, I met with the finance people of course, but I also met with the marketing people and also the salespeople. Everybody said the same thing: 'Whatever job you have to start off with doesn't mean you're going to have that job for a long period of time. Wherever we have the need, we put the right people in the right position, and we hope and expect you can do the best you can for the company.' And that has been true right from the beginning. I came here as an accountant, and they decided that I can do the best job here by taking a marketing role. So for the first couple of years I worked in the micro division in marketing and did a reasonably good job, and then they asked me to move to the West Coast and run part of the marketing department there, which I enjoyed for about fifteen months. And that's when CA started to grow by leaps and bounds and started acquiring big companies, and they decided they needed more help back here in the accounting and financial area. So I worked in sales accounting and also had some treasury responsibility, which I carried for a few years. Then they needed me elsewhere, and I helped to design some of the internal accounting systems for CA. Then they asked me to look at what is going on in the sales side of contracts, to help the salespeople. For a year and a half I had full responsibility for what was booked and what wasn't booked. And now I'm playing the role of internal auditor, running around looking at various pieces of the operations of the company. Six and a half years, five major responsibilities, everything from having 120 people reporting to me to working directly with Tony. And I don't know what I'm going to do tomorrow. [Within four months of this interview, Bob was sent on a three-week audit of operations in the Far East and then returned to be put in charge of sales in a newly acquired division headquartered in Chicago.] By training I'm an accountant, but what I do is what needs to be done. The funny thing is sometimes I get calls from headhunters, we all do, and they think that because I'm doing marketing I'm a marketing person, that's my background, my résumé. I could be in marketing four days and that's what they think, that I'm a professional marketing person. To them that's my training. But it isn't."

In fact, by the time the twenty-first century rolls around, training may itself become a kind of handicap, because a well-trained person is by definition perfectly suited for work that was obsolete when it became a subject for training, or even before. When management guru Peter F. Drucker said in a 1991 *Forbes* magazine interview that "you can get Ph.D.'s quickly, but experience takes time," this wisdom did not go quite far enough. The degreed and the experienced both now suffer under the same disability: according to the qualifications they are most proud of, these are people who know how to handle what *was*, only sometimes are prepared for what *is*, and seldom if ever for what *will be*.

When Charles, who eats his lunches at his desk or around a conference table, decided in late summer he'd had enough afternoon heartburn, he asked Deborah Coughlin if she wouldn't mind spending August finding a replacement caterer for the CA cafeteria. On the surface this makes as much sense as calling in a dentist to dig out the hole for a swimming pool in your backyard: Debbie handles investor relations for CA. She's the person Wall Street analysts and investors call for an explanation of CA's numbers. That's both her training and her experience. So why, of all people, her?

Debbie not only sits about a hundred feet from Charles' office, which makes her handy, but August is traditionally a slack time in the investor relations business. Besides, Debbie makes it a habit every week to bring in home-baked brownies or muffins for

143

her immediate office neighbors. Does that make her perfect for the job of interviewing vendors and negotiating contracts covering the arcane minutiae of industrial catering? Probably not. But somebody had to do it. And how much experience does it take for a capable person to determine if a caterer is suitable? How much experience does it take to talk about insurance with Jay Callanan across the hall or discuss the numbers with Pete Schwartz in finance? What it takes is neither a degree in nutrition nor ten years as manager of a corporate cafeteria. It takes sense. Debbie: "They asked me to do it, so I did it. It was new, a challenge, and I learned a lot along the way." This is not to say suitability, experience, training, and even temperament are not factors, but at best they are coexistent with attitude, general smarts, and trust. Russ: "How I hire? It's off the wall how I hire. It's gut. I'll tell you, when we were building CA development, I brought people in like Gary Lewkowitz and Don Osley. I would talk to them and just get a feeling: this guy seems to be a straight-shooter, he knows his stuff. You ask him some technical questions, but more so, you're looking for the personality. What kind of guy is he?" More often than not, all that good résumé material—the so-called objective criteria we have learned to seek for ourselves and worship in others—just gets eclipsed. Russ: "Does he seem to be a motivated guy? Does he seem to be someone a little crazy who's not going to go home at five o'clock? He's going to work? He's going to get it done? He's going to be more motivated by his work than by what time it is? You know, we have guys, we have them at CA, where if it's five o'clock—and they could be in the middle of writing a sentence or in the middle of writing a line of code—but it's five o'clock, and they've got to get home because they've got to be home for dinner or whatever it is. You don't look for that. I never look for that. I'm looking for the creative type—does this person seem creative, does this person seem to be nuts in terms of the way we work and go for it as a competitor? And that's a big part of it." **Knocked away by simple, subjective interpersonal faith.** Russ: "So in terms of hiring, what I used to do is see a guy like Gary Lewkowitz and say, *I don't want to lose this guy.* Or Don Osley, another very key guy in development. I knew I wanted him. I made him an offer. I said, 'Don, I would like you to start, when can you start?' 'Well, I have to give my other company two weeks' notice.' I said, 'Fine, let me look it up. OK, so you could start December third, that's a Monday. OK, now here is what I would like to offer you,' and I'd give him an offer. 'Well, I would really like to go home and think about it a little bit.' I said, 'Tell you what, I'm going to leave you right here because I don't want to lose you. I'm going to go get a cup of coffee, be back in twenty minutes. I'm going to talk to some people. Give me an answer then.' I wouldn't let him out of the building. I hired him. I wouldn't let him leave until I hired him. I wanted to hire this guy. You know, *now.* No fifty-six reference checks and I'm going to call your sixth-grade teacher and your twelfth-grade teacher and who did you work for last? Instead, you look at people's potential. Look at someone like Arnie, really amazing what he's doing. Did you know he headed up marketing for CA? What the hell does he know about software? He headed up marketing. Now he's heading up sales. He's a lawyer. But you look for potential. First thing, the key thing: whether you trust the guy." **Trust, always that.** Gary Lewkowitz, senior vice president, research and development: "If they don't trust you, why would you want to be here?"

Considering that Wall Street analysts have been known to criticize CA for being, in Tony's words, "a company run by two Chinamen," there are a lot more "Chinamen" than are immedi-

ately apparent. (For an indication of the quality of such analysis, consider that one brilliant commentator used such subtitles in his writeup as "A Step in the Wang Direction" and "Can Two Wangs Do What's Right?") Yes, Charles does have final say and retains tight control over the direction of the company, but the CA system may well be the least command-oriented among major U.S. corporations. Yet it doesn't show. The lines of responsibility are diffused out of sight. Russ: "First thing, the key thing: whether you trust the guy. Do you trust him? Is he a guy who will bullshit you, or it is someone you can trust?" Through frameworks of trust (elliptically stated: I trust you to use your judgment, which I trust, not to make decisions in an area you don't feel you have my trust for), a system of what might be called neural networks extends outward from the center and back again. Ever shifting, ever changing, these relationships have only one constant: Charles and Tony are always available. Blaming Wall Street analysts for missing this point is a little like blaming your hamster for failing at calculus. He doesn't even know it's there.

To be fair, CA's public relations effort is focused on its products, not its corporate image and especially not how the company works. But for those who care to see it, trust and reliance on the voluntary cooperation of others is so intrinsic to the way CA operates that if both Charles and Tony were to disappear, their functions would be carried on without as much as an interregnum hitch. Parallel leadership is built into the system at every level and in every department. In Charles' absence, Tony or Arnie parallel. In Tony's, Charles, Arnie, or Sanjay are there. In Russ's absence, Nancy parallels. And likewise, if both Nancy and Russ are away, others feel confident making decisions. This isn't filling in. This isn't scribbling a notation and taking it up with your boss when she returns from San Diego. This is saying,

146

"I am qualified to make decisions because I am trusted to make them, and I am trusted to make them because I am qualified." Thus, even at the buck-stops-here level, the idea is to have people in place you can trust to get the job, any job, done right.

And to tell you when you're not doing yours. And not only within the inner circle. Pete: "Tell them, 'This is a mistake, we shouldn't be doing that'? Oh, yeah. But when I was at Xerox, you couldn't go up to people at the decision-maker level and say, 'I think you're pissing away a hell of a lot of money on this corporate airplane fleet.' It happens to be one thing I knew a lot about. 'And if you would take your yacht off the expense account, it might be a little more profitable here.' You didn't do that." It holds true at many removes. Pete: "At CA a salesman can walk into Charles' office and say, 'I think this is a screwed-up way of marketing this product.'" In fact, at all of them.

Yet there is another side to trust: to succeed, it must be mutual. When earlier we discussed trust, we looked at the concept from the point of view of management, which needs people it can trust. But trustworthy people have to be able to do some trusting of their own. Judy Holt: "Columbus Day weekend or not, the work's got to be done. You make room for it, and if you have to give up your weekend, you're doing it because it has to be done. You want to get it done. They need it." Yet the employee who works his tail off for an immediate superior and is then robbed of the credit is not only a staple of popular fiction—the reality is a commonplace. Jo Ann Sciachetano, administrative assistant: "There are two good reasons we all come in like this on a Columbus Day weekend. Saturday I was in from two-thirty to seven-thirty, Sunday from ten-thirty to seven-thirty. Today is Columbus Day, and Judy, Barbara, and I will probably put in another day and a half. We'll work into the night, maybe until next morning. The first reason is they need you. There's a deadline on this project, and everyone who can is asked to come in. You want to help, and you don't want to say no. The other is that it's recognized. At the end of the year they know what you've done. It's remembered." **Anyone who has had anything to do with traditional corporate life viscerally understands the compelling and ultimately corrupting premise that builds mistrust into the system.** Barbara Boland, administrative assistant: "There are people in the company who say, 'I would never do that. I would never stay and work late and through the weekend like that.' But it gives you a sense of accomplishment. You're part of something. And if Jo Ann didn't come in and Judy didn't come and I didn't come in, who do they have? These are people you work with and trust, people you like. I wouldn't leave them in a bind like that. Anyway, after a while you get your second wind. You yawn a few times, that's all." **Because in the traditional hierarchical company a manager assumes the value of his subordinates. Like a feudal lord, he is measured not by their productivity but by their number. But at CA a manager is measured by the productivity of those who report to him—and often, in even sharper contrast to the traditional model, by their productivity divided by their number: the two standard measurements within the company are cost per employee and revenue per employee. In this way CA has clearly established a direct disincentive to hire a great many people to do a piece of work: a manager who can do with 12 instead of 112 not only affects the bottom line but is in the pleasant position of having discovered what Karl Marx might grudgingly have called the most efficient means of production—had he thought of it.** Pete: "We've got four people in payroll paying close to five thousand." **Rather than merely producing work, the CA manager produces producers.**

IV. Profitable

The incentive for these producers must be immediate. Though Charles from the beginning reorganized CA to get the best working combination of people every chance he could (and now, even with nearly eight thousand on the payroll, he still does it as often as he dares), he quickly found there was another good reason to keep shuffling the deck: the need to reward frequently is met by the need to be frequently rewarded. Reuven: "I don't know of any other place where you can really start at the bottom and in no time go straight up, based definitely not on the time you spend in the company but on the potential you show. That's something that's really amazed me again and again and again. I mean, I can't complain about my career at IBM, but if I'd stayed there, I'd definitely be a few floors lower than I am here. And it's so clear here you can see it: the young people who come in here, you can take them, if they show fresh thinking, and move them fast enough before they become the kind of organizational creatures who are just going to contribute to more bureaucracy and less efficiency and so forth. So the faster you do it, the faster you can recognize and reward. If the person has potential, he or she is going to contribute much earlier and much more." So how to reward, the bane of almost any management scheme, became a problem that solved itself, once the alternatives were thought through. Though CA rewards good work with good money, to simply add to the paycheck once (a bonus) amounts to a tip, a gratuity that all but screams that the person has done more than is

149

necessary. That isn't the message CA wants to send. On the other hand, to add to the paycheck permanently is to reward someone forever for doing what he or she did yesterday. Traditional corporate compensation thus keeps falling between the ignominy of the tip and the ineconomy of the sinecure. Both are destructive; the swing between them perhaps more so.

Nothing better illustrates how CA deals with compensation than the company's monthly Best Idea competition. This is little different from any common corporate suggestion box except that at CA the winner gets no cash, no weekend at a hotel, no electric coffee maker. The winner simply gets cited on CA bulletin boards for Best Idea and—up to the time of its move to new corporate headquarters—a month's use of the parking space next to Charles' right outside the front door at 711 Stewart Avenue, where thousands of CA people were able to take note of it as they entered and left every day. "To: ALL GARDEN CITY EMPLOYEES. From: ANTHONY WANG. Subject: BEST IDEA. It's nice to see a lot of good suggestions this month. We are fortunate to have a winner and first runner-up for the month of October. The winner is Bill Tinkler for his idea of reminding each and every employee at CA that regardless of job function, we are sales people. Every one of us contributes to the sales effort in one way or the other. All of us from time to time deal with or are in contact with a client or potential client and occasionally come across a potential sales opportunity and unfortunately may not know what to do with this valuable information. Bill as an example works in Level I support and has on more than one occasion learned of a potential sales opportunity and unfortunately could not find the proper sales person to whom to provide this valuable information. Bill's idea is to provide a simple and easy-to-use

150

mechanism to facilitate the communication of leads from non-sales personnel to sales personnel. Bill also suggested that some real examples of the types of opportunities that he has come across be shared with the readers of this memo so that you too can recognize sales opportunities. [List of examples.] When it comes to simple and easy-to-use, Mr. Simple and Easy himself, Paul Lancey, Senior Vice President of Sales, has volunteered to personally take on the responsibility of making sure that each and every sales opportunity brought to his attention will be immediately distributed to the appropriate District Sales Manager. In addition, he has agreed, if appropriate, to keep the originator of the lead informed as to its status. Paul can be reached at extension 7298, or if Paul is not available, please contact Barbara Stordeur or Monica Stordeur [more sisters] at extensions 7652 and 7278. . . . Paul encourages all of us nonsales types including myself to help the sales effort whenever and however possible. You can never tell how some innocent information exchanged between a client and a CA employee can help make a good quarter into a great quarter. THINK SALES AND KEEP THE SALES LEADS COMING! Our first runner-up this month is Mickey Ward. Mickey's idea is to use a phone prompting system for the Computer Services Hotline. All too often, when there is a rare systems problem, we all call the Computer Systems Hotline at the same time. This causes the queue to be filled up while we wait for the next available operator. The phone prompting system will allow the caller to listen to prerecorded messages dealing with such things as systems problems and stats as well as systems news and other vital up-to-date information without having to talk to an operator. The new procedure will save the callers and technicians valuable time that is currently used relaying messages about systems problems and answering the same question numerous times. This procedure is not meant to be the solution for every problem—therefore one of the choices on the phone prompting system will be for an operator. J. P. Scarisbrick will implement the phone prompting system as soon as possible. As soon as the system is set up, information about the new procedures will be distributed. As the winner, Bill gets the use of the parking place in front of 711 Stewart Avenue for the month of November. As for our first runner-up, Mickey gets the recognition and all the related benefits of being first runner-up. [Asked later what these related benefits are, Tony offered a smile.] Congratulations, Bill and Mickey, and thanks to everyone who contributed ideas this month."

Don't let the relaxed diction and ain't-it-swell tone of these posted notices fool you. The message is crystal clear and just as cutting: (a) you're paid to think to the best of your ability, so don't expect to be tipped for revealing that you can think even better but normally don't, and (b) keep thinking this well and pretty soon there will be a place for you—and not just your car—among those who run CA.

It follows that CA's idea of reward is more work at better pay. But to be able to offer this kind of incentive means making the corporate structure so amorphous that shooting stars have something to shoot for. Replacing the pyramid is thus not merely something practical from the point of view of those controlling the structure, but from the point of view of those who are that structure.

For people who can leap to the top, climbing the corporate ladder is nothing less than torture. They not only need room to fly, but comfort on the ascent. Example? Before CA acquired the company, Sanjay Kumar's salary at Uccel was $100,000. Four years later? Leaving aside stock options, that salary is $380,000. Of course, Sanjay *is* almost thirty now.

V. Endless

Not a complaint. If the symbol of the twentieth-century corporation is the clean desk, with everything under control and, at the end of each day, all work neatly completed, the symbol of the twenty-first-century corporation will be its antithesis, the messy desk that will not go away. Piled high with incoming messages that must be answered, with projects that may never be completed because successful projects breed new ones that often promise greater success—to say nothing of ideas, plans, doodles, and leftovers from lunch—CA's dream desk is IBM's worst nightmare. Reuven: "IBM has a clean-desk policy, and when I worked there, you won't believe this, every time before I could take a trip, travel anywhere, they wouldn't let me go until I cleaned up my desk. My desk was always full of papers. The ugliest. So I found a very easy way to deal with this. Before I left I threw everything in a closet, and when I came back, I put it all back on my desk. At IBM, to have a desk like this is definitely a point against you. It really is a sickness with them, an absolutely neat, tidy desk. Here things come in and things go out, and when you have things sitting on your desk, it's not necessarily a sign that you can't deal with it. It's very easy to say yes or no with great authority and then move it. But I know from what I do that there are certain problems that you look at and say, 'I'll think about this,' and you put it aside. After all, what am I being paid for, my ability to move paper off my desk or my ability to make the right decisions? So of course I'll have a messy desk. Here everyone has a messy desk." But there is more to endlessness than mess:

[a] **It is without temporal boundaries.** A travel administrator: "Most things around here are a snappy-do. Very rarely does someone come over and say, 'You have a year to take care of this. Handle it for me.' Everything is immediate. Everything is last-minute. Everything is late. There is no next week. It's either today or maybe tomorrow morning. If I did a computer scan on all the airline reservations in this company, there would be nobody traveling this coming Monday. The whole company would be traveling between now and Friday. If I scanned the travel system, all the trips planned would be planned for tomorrow. What's today, Tuesday? Most of the trips would be for Tuesday night, Wednesday, Thursday, and a few things for Friday. Monday? Nothing. Two weeks from now? I'm telling you we don't even plan for Monday. And when I'm talking about nothing, I'm literally talking about nothing—less than one percent. Next week? Nobody knows next week. Charles wouldn't know what he is doing next week. Yeah, he could look at his calendar and tell you he might be here or he might be there, but he isn't there next week until he gets to next week. That's how the company operates. Everything's today." **CA refuses to be limited to an inflexible calendar when the objective world, the one outside, keeps changing so fast.** The same travel administrator: "There *is* scheduling—there has to be scheduling. But people won't talk to me about a meeting in March until at least January. They will not talk to me. We argue about it. 'I need information, I need planning.' They say, 'The quarter has to be over.' I say, 'But, I need some basic information.' They say, 'Make it up.' " **Tomorrow's projects and responsibilities may have nothing at all to do with today's or yesterday's or tomorrow's plans, to say nothing of expectations and hopes.** The travel administrator: "Whatever they say, I'd have to change it, so it doesn't matter. Really it's probably better. They're going to

change it anyway, so if we wait until January, I have less to change."

[b] It is endless in the sense that it is relentless. It won't be quieted, won't go away—not least because there are no job descriptions. Gary: "Everybody does everything. We don't have people who say, 'I don't do that—that's not my job.' I've never heard that. It's not something people say. Whatever has to get done, whatever it takes to get it done, we're going to get it done." That is to say, no job limitations. Reuven: "Just the idea of product-owner, especially the second half of it. When you're in charge of everything, it's very hard to find an excuse that says, 'Well, someone else didn't do it.' Because you know someone else didn't do it is just the reason why you've got to do it, even if it's not what you're doing now. It doesn't work, so you've got to." In any normal corporation each individual is in charge of a small part of a large product, with the overall responsibility either in no one's hands or in the hands of someone sitting at a clean desk with flowers on it at the end of a long corridor. At CA the success or failure of each product is considered to be in the hands of each person. There is no shrugging off, because the goal is not getting through the day by fulfilling a list of functions, but doing anything that must be done. Nancy: "CA developers, CA people, they kind of own things. I don't have to sit on top of them and say you've got to call the client back, you've got to look at follow-up. Like this mailing thing—it's not a development task to follow up on the mailing. Our job is supposed to be done when we cut the tape or write the piece of technical collateral, but they just go and do it. They understand that if it doesn't leave the mailroom then it doesn't do anybody any good. They will own that kind of stuff, and I don't have to remind them. They'll just do

it, and if they see a problem, they know how to escalate. They won't just stop and do nothing." **And doing enough of it today doesn't allow CA people to forget about it for a week, because it keeps coming.** Nancy: "It's weird, because we do get people to go home, take vacations, and so on, but a lot of that work-until-you-drop is self-induced. It's not demanded. They just want to see their products succeed. That's ultimately the biggest charge: to see that what you've done is successful. So part of my job as a manager is to make sure what they do is within reason, that they don't get too extreme about it." **So you have to keep coming as well.** Don: "One of the things you learn from the day you start working here is that whatever Charles tells you today, he will change it tonight, and then he'll change it tomorrow. That's probably why I'm comfortable here. I don't like things that stay the same. I'm comfortable with that, and in this company everything changes all the time." **So you'd better like it.**

[c] It is endless because the line that divides people from their employment is erased: to the extent it is individually possible, the person *becomes* the work. Not possible? In the jungles of South America the last primitive hunter-gatherers are active throughout the day but are said to do no work at all. Though they spend their entire lives taking care of what we would call business (at least until they become "civilized" by missionaries), the languages of these Stone Age people normally do not include so much as a single word that reflects the concept of work. This is because what they do to make a living has not yet been departmentalized out of their "real" lives.

If this idea strikes a chord of memory in the reader, but one which is difficult to identify, the reason is veiled but simple: at one time, each of us was an uncivilized stone-ager, except that

157

the preferred term was teenager. Teenagers and of course younger children are unconflicted by the dual loyalties of work life and personal life. By the time we complete our formal education, a new person comes into existence, and that person, if he is like most of us, lives two lives, cut off from each other and usually competitive. A senior developer: "Most people in the company know that "X" and I live together, and without naming names, because it can complicate things outside the company. This kind of situation isn't uncommon at CA. The result is you don't have a private life. You have hours in which you're together away from the office, but even then you're part of CA. Last night I got home about eight with a takeout pizza. "X" was in the bedroom. The house was dark, and she called down to me when I opened the front door, 'I'm up here,' which is nice to hear after a long day's work. So I climbed the stairs with my pizza, and there she is in bed wearing not much more than a big smile and about twenty different stacks of papers from the office spread all around. I had to laugh, you know, because I recognized right away that I wasn't really surprised. Most of the time I give her the same deal. But when you think about it, it's just what's normal for us." We need not live two separate lives. "X": "You don't think of work interfering with your sleep or your love life—you think of it as life."

From the moment we decide that what we do is different from what we are, we have created work in one or both of its pejorative senses: a job, which is limited in potential, or labor, which is aimless. Either way, there is a sense of compulsion; in both we are forced to do what is not within us. But if we're lucky enough so that what we do is what we are, ah, then we join the tribal hunter, the cop, the priest, the drug dealer, the scholar, the explorer, and the few others whose businesses are their lives.

Getting used to this may or may not be easy, but at CA there is an acculturating factor—family as a network of relationships based on trust. Mike: "They have to feel we are in some way trying to make this a real family, just like you would help your brother or sister. I think they feel that way. Because we try to instill, as corny as it may sound, a brother-and-sister–type routine, saying, 'Hey, listen, this guy is still working on this project. If I can help him, I'll ask him if he wants me to stay.' " The same mechanism that identifies trustworthy people among family and friends and brings them into CA is also the mechanism that identifies and acculturates complete outsiders.

Significantly and uniquely, CA reaches so far out that its corridors make the United Nations Secretariat look provincial. Especially with technical personnel, CA likes to move employees from country to country, so that in many offices it is possible to stroll past cubicles where in the same aisle programmers can be overheard heatedly discussing software solutions in French, Italian, Hebrew, and Chinese. There is direct benefit to CA, of course, because each person returns to his home office with advanced knowledge and increased sophistication. But there is a kind of ramified benefit as well, because the learning process is two way. The gain can be significant. (Whatever other barriers remain between the U.S. and Japan, for instance, it's clear that Japanese automakers have hired many more Americans than Chrysler, GM, and Ford have hired Japanese, who know a thing or two of value to Detroit.) There simply is no market that is local anymore. To serve the needs of this world market requires individuals who feel at home in it, like Mario Pelleschi. Mario started at CA Switzerland, transferred to Germany, became managing director of CA Brazil and now runs CA operations in Germany, Austria, and Switzerland.

159

Unlike the standard, button-down American multinational corporation, which dispatches American executives to colonize divisions abroad, CA often brings non-Americans to the United States either permanently or for a tour of duty. Nothing better expresses the openness of CA than the sight of Charles, a Chinese-American, shepherding twenty or so managers out the door at Islandia—people from Australia, Austria, Belgium, Brazil, Canada, Denmark, Finland, France, Germany, Holland, Hong Kong, Israel, Italy, New Zealand, Norway, Singapore, Spain, Sweden, Switzerland, the United Kingdom—all of them on the way to an Italian restaurant. Each of these individuals—like David J. Wardle, the former Hong Kong policeman who joined as a salesman and helped build CA's American sales operation—began as an outsider. Whether from Athens, Greece, or Athens, Ohio, there CA employees start out being nobody's cousin and carry no credentials of built-up trust. Mike: "You get them to buy this idea of family by showing them that you are there for them. Where some families have problems is they don't have this cohesion. Here, when somebody has a problem, you try to say, 'What's the problem, how can we help you?' Whether it's a personal or a business problem, I think that's what we try, and once you do that enough times to somebody, he or she catches on and says, 'Hey, that was pretty nice. Now how am I going to return that favor?'" So trust must be created, moving outward toward the unknown, the untried, the unqualified. Mike: "And they see their next person, and they build on that. It's not perfect, but I've got that in a lot of people in what I call my core. I have a core. If I can keep that core, I can always build off that. If I build one or two more people off that core every year, great. If I build five or six, great. That's what I try to do, have a core. You know exactly what? If I ask them to wash the floor tonight, my core will do that.

It is not an original idea here. That's how Charles works with me. He built a core and I'm part of it. So now I'm building a core." **And trust makes them qualified.** Mike: "I got an e-mail on our system from a district manager. We had a situation where the client, a big department store chain, ordered something from CA and got the wrong thing shipped, not the fault of the shipper, my people, the fault of the way the order was put in. Whose fault it was is not important. They ordered something again, got it wrong again, not the fault of the shipper. The district sales manager called up and said, 'Look, the client is fuming at me. We know it's not your fault, but what can we do? They need it today.' Now, all on her own, our distribution person says OK, I will drive this tape directly to the client's local store and have them—because they have their own little distribution network within the chain—have them get the tape to the right person the same day. Well, nobody asked that, nobody said anything. The distribution person could just have said, 'My job is to put it in the box, period. What I'll do is put it into the box, and when it gets there, it gets there.' So here is an e-mail saying this is what one of your people did and I want to tell you this is us that screwed up, and this is how we screwed up, and then we screwed it up again and called, and this woman said, 'I'll drive it to the local store.' I mean, the district manager in sales—works for Arnie—all on his own said, 'I want to tell you we entered it wrong, we blew it. Somebody else did it, they blew it—not your people. We called up again and said, "We are in big trouble, what are we going to do?"' And I'm talking about an eighteen-, nineteen-thousand-dollar-a-year person, who's got a million things to do during the day. They ship out a thousand orders a week on Long Island. They don't have time to redo things three times. They don't have time to

161

make personal deliveries. I didn't tell her to do that. Her boss didn't tell her to do it. She just did it. I don't know many corporations where they'd even think to look for a solution and then actually do it. Isn't that something?" **Isn't that something?**

VI. Contractual Selflessness

It is, but by any normal standard of business behavior, there's something seriously wiggy here. Things are not supposed to work out this way.

Remember, initially we reasoned that to produce as much as possible we need help, so let's get people we trust. This calls for family. But since there's a limit to the qualified people we know, let's bring in strangers and make them family. To do that—to help them become people we can trust—we've got to make them understand they can trust us. To make them trust us, we've got to be less interested in our own welfare and more interested in theirs: we've got to become selfless. Because we have important work to accomplish, we act selflessly in order to teach others to act selflessly.

This may sound like business Zen—do not what you must, do what you don't and the work will get done—but it is merely the basis of a simple promise: work as we work and you shall be rewarded. Reduced one step further, this becomes an even simpler contract: be as we are and you shall be us.

If this sounds familiar, it's because it is, in the most literal sense of the word. It is the basis for almost everyone's private life: it is family building, the self-intensifying process that strengthens and enlarges families. As do families, CA uses it to bring in trustworthy individuals. And just as the process erases the boundaries that separate an individual's family and personal lives, so it does with a person's corporate and personal lives.

At a birthday celebration for Mike Picker's infant son, most of the guests were folks who work at CA, and most of those were family. The family was not so much extended as ramified; as many as were cousins and as many as were colleagues, the greater number of either was both. The line between personal and business life had been wiped away.

At CA's annual picnic and other celebrations, there is the same peculiar sense of gathered family, clan, tribe. When it numbers in the thousands, this may seem to be one unwieldy family, and some of its members will have to be introduced to others. But each person will be directly related to people directly related to them. If to the stranger there is the vague feeling of being uninitiated, outside, temporary, those within the CA group feel just the opposite: initiated, inside, permanent.

For a family this is pretty much on the mark, because permanence is precisely what distinguishes family from all other human associations. So long as these people do not in some way betray the family, we accept them and deal with them as they are. And as with any good family that is capable of expansive growth, those brought in from outside share the same warmth as those who have been there from the beginning.

Families grow three ways: through procreation (children), through agglutination (sons- and daughters-in-law), and through adoption. In terms of the work force, this translates to, respectively, growth through primary hiring, through what we'll call chain hiring (Tony Wang brings in Arnie Mazur, who brings in

Mike Picker, who brings in Bob Toth, and so on), and through the familiation of outsiders, like Sanjay, whose companies were acquired. No matter how they are hired, everyone shares the same benefits of the family, and (aside from death), the same ways out. Sometimes it happens that people go their own way, like Abraham Poznanski, CA's long-time CFO, whose turn to Orthodox Judaism caused him to be uncomfortable in the corporate framework he had helped build.* Abe: "Basically I still consider myself part of the family. If I were going to work for somebody and not be on my own, I wouldn't want to work for anybody else." But this is a rare exception. Normally there is only one way to leave a family standing up.

And that is through dishonor. You dishonor the family by betraying it, which explains why CA attempts to maintain a policy of not rehiring people who quit (and in those specific exceptions never at a salary higher than when they left, lest those who stayed suffer by comparison), or by dishonoring yourself. The penalty for acting dishonorably at CA is the loss of employment; but for merely not being able to do the job? At CA there always seems to be a place for someone whose talents do not match his hopes. Yet for someone whose efforts fall below his ambitions, there is only a one-way ticket out the front door. Tony: "If they don't care about CA, I don't want them here anyway." Family is why the overgrown boys who play nose-buster basketball with Charles are a different breed from the traditional boss's golfing partners, who are notoriously willing to lose at any price. The CA guys are simply unable to make a distinction between

---

*Footnote: Four years after he left in 1988, Abe rejoined CA. Some families you can't quit.

165

their social and business lives—because there isn't any. Arguing
with Charles about the wisdom or stupidity of a business move
is simply the daytime equivalent of attempting to jump-shoot
past his upstretched arms. There may be friction because of it,
but you don't get thrown out of the family for trying to warn
your brother-in-law against investing his life's savings in Norwe-
gian banana futures. You betray him if you don't.

Successful people in successful families establish a contract
within the family. The terms and scope of such agreements may
vary from situation to situation and change over time, but the
essential element is a willingness to blend the personal ego into
a greater ego, to desire and work for some greater good without
compromising the dignity and integrity of the individual. In good
families people work together—contractually.

The work contract at CA is rarely stated and is not written, nor
need it be. Because the contract is not with the company—
whose form keeps changing while the stationery stays the
same—but with the people who hired you and those you hire—
and with those, assuming the constant reorganization that is the
hallmark of CA, to whom you later report and who report to you.
Bob: "The worst punishment for me would be feeling I'd let
them down." This is not methodology. Jay: "It's your job, but
it's also your life." It is character. Methods may change—in
fact, at CA they are bound to—but the underlying character of
the corporation remains the same.

VII. Ethics

Contractual selflessness is an accurate description of what underlies CA's corporate character—up to a point. But without one other element CA would fall into the trap of any family-type organization whose standards are insufficiently high to keep it from self-destructing. When you manage by results, the only occasion for a postmortem is when they are poor. Since there is normally little to no interest in how things get done when they get done well, there is always the danger that the means are thoroughly unjustifiable. The Mafia works well as a family organization, for instance, but in its relations outside the family it is, as a matter of principle, rigorously unethical.

With one standard inside the company and another standard outside, a kind of behavioral Gresham's Law intervenes: bad standards drive out good. The same standards that apply outside the family sooner or later take hold within.

As a matter of survival if not preference, CA has enshrined ethical behavior as its single standard.

This ethical standard explains why CA purchasing practices drive suppliers to the wall, but never through it. It is why CA refuses to consider not spending a million dollars a year to keep paying for employees' breakfasts. It is why in bargaining over the price of an acquisition Sanjay will use persuasion, timing, and charm to get a price the sellers never even considered.

Sanjay: "This deal, they had a figure in their heads of about seven million bucks. Seven million was a number that if you plopped down seven million in cash, you could walk away with the company, which was basically one product. Nine would have been like Christmas for them, four and a half would have been the very bottom. I kind of got that from talking and discussion. I do a lot of that, face to face. So then I come back with a number that says, 'I'll give you a million up front and some minimum every year,' so that they could end up with two and a half million guaranteed, but probably they'd make a lot more. So they were there and I was here. Imagine the negative reaction, but that's expected. They go away, they come back." **Sanjay knows that once the deal is struck, it is cement.** Sanjay: "With some reposturing and negotiating and talking about what essentially the business could do down the road, they settle for the royalty. The net effect is essentially a lot below what they would have really liked to have walked away with." **Because there will be no replacing the spirit of the agreement for the letter.** Sanjay: "You see, we can offer them a vision of what we can do with the product that no one else can." **So the letter must be right.** Arnie: "When we opened our office in Israel, one of the first people I hired was a controller. We quickly came to terms on the salary—in Israel an American salary goes a long way—and shook hands on the deal. Next day she comes to see me at the hotel and says she doesn't like the deal she agreed to the day before. She had compared notes with one of the other managers I signed up and discovered he was getting a car and she wasn't. She insisted on a car. I told her she not only wasn't getting the car—she wasn't getting the job. Then she said, 'OK, I don't want the car.' I said, 'I'm sorry, but you've

shown me CA doesn't want you,' and I hired someone else.
A deal is a deal." It may be hard, but it must be honest.

Nothing better illustrates this naked disregard for the way business is usually done than what happens after an acquisition, when some percentage of the acquired staff must be let go. Not only has Charles himself always evaluated the file of each of the acquired people individually, which may run into thousands of names, but each person is these days interviewed by CA people, each is given the benefit of absolute consideration, and each is told point-blank whether he does or does not have a future at CA.

In 1988, a year after CA had acquired Uccel and layed off a large percentage of the Texas company's work force in one fell swoop, a similar scene was played out in the atrium of the Princeton headquarters of ADR. At noon of yet another day frought with the fear, loathing, and distrust that accompany any acquisition, Charles stood before the reluctant survivors, those chosen to join the new company. (ADR employees who had not made the cut had been informed earlier that same morning.) The mood was uniformly unpretty: most of the survivors expected to be fired at some later date. So when Charles took the podium holding up a pair of sneakers, it was one of those moments when anger, fear, and the agony of uncertainty give way—are simply displaced, if only for the moment—by simple curiosity.

CA people had been scratching around for hours trying to find someone with a spare pair of shoes; sneakers is what they had found. "If any of you believes that next month or next quarter CA is going to inaugurate another round of firings," Charles said, "forget it. From this moment on, you are CA people, working under the same benefits and conditions as anyone else at CA. There will be no next round of firings." He tossed the sneakers on the atrium floor, one after the other. "There is," he said, "no other shoe."

And there wasn't.

Part Four:

Future

I. Assets

When Mark Twain wrote that "there are lies, damn lies and statistics," he might just as well have gone whole hog and included annual reports. As a snapshot of corporate health, stability, and integrity, these are ordinarily about as accurate as a photo chosen at random from anybody's family album, where what or who is in the picture is often not as significant as what or who isn't. Think of photos of happy families just before the calamity of separation and divorce; dad's mistress is nowhere to be seen, nor are mom's hidden bottles of booze, the neighborhood drug dealer, the psychiatrist.

The photos never reveal the triumphs, either—neither the current ones nor those on the way. All they really prove is that you cannot trust something large, subtle, and complex to a snapshot. In a world of annual reports—corporate snapshots that tell less than the whole story—few annuals are less revealing than CA's.

Certainly the columns of figures are neatly balanced, and the heads and subheads accurately divvy up assets and liabilities the way other annual reports do. In CA's case it is probably done with greater satisfaction for the shareholder, because CA is as financially conservative as it is operationally radical. It would have to be. Think of how a heavy keel steadies a racing boat. As of this writing, CA's balance sheet holds no debt and about $250 million in cash—about as strong as possible in a time of highly leveraged companies panting to pay off onerous short-term obligations so as to be able to survive until the day they must deal with even heavier long-term liabilities.

On the face of it, CA's assets are no different from the quantitative common denominators that appear on everyone else's balance sheet: cash, marketable securities, receivables, inventories, real estate, computer equipment, furnishings, and of course, the products the company has developed or acquired. These assets for the fiscal year ending March 1992 will probably come to about $2 billion, though asset valuation, as any good accountant will tell you, is always more subjective than the valuation of liabilities: assets are what you say you own; liabilities, unless misstated, live in a more objective reality. When CA lists its assets, the one that is not mentioned and which is unquantifiable under accepted accounting standards is the one that sets CA apart. That asset is its people and the process of which they are a part.

Whether there will come a day when we'll figure out how to account for this type of asset is unknown. In theory it might be possible to establish a formula for the value of individuals, based on prior performance and dollar value of their responsibility, or according to salary (on the premise that you wouldn't pay someone several hundred thou a year unless he or she is worth it). On the other hand, most companies do just that, and it has been known to happen as well at CA, which has from time to time also put its faith and its money in turkeys. The difference? By constantly reorganizing, CA is able to discover the turkeys quickly and move them into more appropriate jobs in or out of the company.

Our problem becomes even more complicated when we realize that it is not simply the value of individuals we are talking about, but individuals in combination—and even those combinations in combination. At this point there would not be much sense in going on, except for the familiar thought that perhaps the problem itself must be reengineered.

Essentially what we are looking for when we attempt to evaluate a company is not its performance in the past but in the future. In the wrong hands the strongest balance sheet is useless: assets may be misallocated or underemployed or just ignored; liabilities may be poorly managed. Likewise, the most impressive income statement is subject to distortion, whether on the part of the observer, the company itself, or as a function of the peculiarities of its business. For example, CA's first-quarter revenues are always its lowest—the strenuous sales activity at the end of the previous year tends to drain the pipeline at the beginning of the next. Who is to say when the last great quarter may truly be the last? Things change, both within a company and without; dealing with the former in reaction to the latter is what this book has been about.

II. Liabilities

So if we are talking about a twenty-first century in which change will be even further accelerated, certitude is not going to be something easily come by. 'Going by track record alone is richly unpromising—you might as well go on faith. And faith, as we shall see, is an easily destabilized commodity.

Though CA dominates in the kind of software that runs data centers, it is hardly a presence in PCs. Its modest sales of micro software actually dropped last year by 10 percent. This is troubling even if we remain skeptical about the conventional wisdom that sees the end of the line for the IBM mainframe and the midrange machine (and the software systems that run on them), because something is going to have to coordinate the flood of information that ever-increasing numbers of interconnected supercharged PCs are capable of producing. But there is little doubt that happy hour at Café Mainframe is over. From now on, all drinks are going to be full price. Whether or not the mainframe market is shrinking, flat, or just doomed to much slower growth, the fact is that CA owns so much of it that really impressive revenue figures are going to have to come from elsewhere. That elsewhere is generally considered to be software for PCs.

This all but begs the question of why CA did not enter PC software earlier. It did. Certainly in Europe CA sales of micro software are more than respectable: its PC accounting program is a leader for small businesses in many countries; in the United

Kingdom CA's spreadsheet program outsells Lotus. Yet in the United States, the home of PC software, success has been elusive. CA tried. Charles: "We were in there first before everyone else, but we screwed it up. In the early eighties, just before the IBM PC came out, I had my technical guys studying what was already out, playing with it, and then when IBM brought out the PC, we bought one of the first machines. I said, 'Look, the fastest way to get in is let's get a successful PC software company.' We acquired a company in California. First mistake, we didn't consolidate it into the rest of CA. They told me the micro business was different, so I didn't put my own people in it. The acquired company never became part of CA." And tried. Charles: "They had their own sales and their own marketing—nothing could get done. Six years ago I said, 'Guys, we own twenty percent of the spreadsheet market, now let's just clone Lotus. Whatever you've got that's better, great, but just clone Lotus.' They said, 'Yeah, that's a good idea, Charles,' but it never got done. The guys wouldn't do it. They didn't buy off on the philosophy. I could have worked with them if they were here, but they were in California and I was working through several layers. They never would clone it. Quattro Pro cloned it and today owns twenty-four percent of the spreadsheet market, we own less than five percent, and Lotus pretty much owns the rest. There are mistakes like that on and on and on. Every decision got bastardized." And tried. Charles: "We got together and we agreed. Just like we have product-owner meetings, all the micro guys sat down together and agreed. But they changed it. Some had legitimate reasons and some not, but it was plain bastardized until it was worthless." With little reward. Charles: "I picked the wrong guys, the wrong horses to ride. I picked them wrong until this last year—when I picked them wrong again. I did it again! I said to myself, 'Wang, you must be some sort of idiot. These are the wrong guys.' It was the games again, all that political bull. I don't work well that way.' **Charles even used people he trusted to head it up.** Charles: "I don't know what happens to them out there. I appointed my own guys, from within CA, and the same thing happened. They get alfalfa sprouts in their brain out there. I think they shoot up with avocados. It's unbelievable. One of my guys became so ineffective, one of my main guys." **These too turned out to be duds.** Charles: "So when none of this worked, I said, *No—I'm not letting them stay out there on their own anymore. I'm going to deal with it the same way I deal with all acquisitions. I'm going to acquire the company. CA is going to acquire CA's micro division. We're going to go through it the same way as if we are acquiring an outside company, bring in new management, clean it up top to bottom."* **So is CA's poor showing in the PC market up to now a failure?**

III. Balance

To call it a failure, we would have to say that Microsoft, which dominates PC software, failed at mainframe software.* The truth is that CA has simply not been a PC software company.

In at least one instance this self-limiting determination has led to the kind of situation that a lesser company might find embarrassing: in the desk of one CA manager sits the original software for WordPerfect, which became America's number one word-processing software. Before its success, it was offered to CA for a song. CA chose not to sing. Failure?

---

*To compare Microsoft to CA in this regard is to seriously misunderstand the only true vehicle for the creation of wealth: industry. Microsoft's software revenue base remains its fortuitous ownership of the MS-DOS operating system for PCs, acquired from another company when Microsoft chairman William Gates learned IBM was looking for just such a system. Because IBM settled on MS-DOS, the system became standard with nearly every basic IBM and IBM-clone PC sold. Not only did Microsoft not develop MS-DOS, but no marketing skills have been involved: the program simply comes with PCs as a prerequisite for their use. This is a bit like buying the patent to the shoelace at a time when the Bootmakers Guild lets you know it is about to drop buckles. What we're talking about may be profitable, but it is not industry. It is investment. In a decade William Gates' three thousand much-heralded programmers have produced little more than Windows. Whatever the merits of this product, without the passive profits from the sale by PC manufacturers of MS-DOS bundled with their hardware, there would be no Windows—and probably no Microsoft.

It could be classified as such only if we ignore the possibility that every minus may well have a counterbalancing plus. For example, consider these characteristic observations on CA attributes—from both sides:

• An inbred, self-reliant company like CA may miss opportunities because it hires from within; fresh thinking never enters at the top. Other companies—Microsoft is one of them—hire outside technology consultants to recommend new products, or they establish committees. How to explain then that Microsoft has on the market only a handful of products? CA has brought out hundreds. Charles: "We're supposed to be the experts in the software business, right? If I don't have collectively the wisdom of close to eight thousand software experts at CA, what do I have?" Instead of reacting to policy recommendations from those who think they know, CA responds to the best single stimulus there is: the market.

• Doesn't such exaggerated self-reliance provide a fertile ground for mistakes? Hell, yes. Here's an ad in a major business magazine headlined: "Our Software Is Behind Almost Every Company In This Magazine. . . . Big or small, young or old, the companies of the Business Week Global 1000 seem to agree on one thing. Computer Associates Software." Great stuff; unfortunately the business magazine was *Forbes*. Or take the international newsletter put out by CA's Product Integration Group, the notorious Pigs. Called Pigpen, of course, it turned out to be offensive to Muslims. Charles: "If it was a big mistake, we would have changed it right away. That's probably the difference and explains why we do things so much on our own, why we don't fly things by a consultant or a committee. Instead of flying it by people, we actually do it. That's how we are able to execute very

180

quickly, and if it's wrong, we change it." Small mistakes are part of the price for being able to make big decisions quickly.

• A company that refuses to "play the Wall Street game," as Tony puts it, is fated to be at a serious disadvantage with professional speculators. From four current randomly chosen analyst reports: "The stock investors love to hate"; "Management remains unwilling to discuss"; "Management was not particularly helpful in providing guidance on either current business trends or estimates for the upcoming year"; "CA president Anthony Wang, aside from providing some revenue, expense and balance sheet details, did not comment in any depth on how the company is doing." Then again a company totally dependent on the goodwill of Wall Street is likely to forget what it should be doing, which is creating wealth, not attracting it.*

• When a major but irresponsible industry publication reported that CA was about to close down its European companies and deal through agents, was the damage worth the savings accumulated by not having someone on the payroll to control the damage before it occurred? CA's European operation standing alone would be the world's third-largest software company, an increasingly profitable part of CA that contributes close to half of its revenues. Shouldn't the press be kept informed? Is snubbing the press a good idea for a company like CA? Probably not,

---

*When, in the depths of a recession, CA turned in a record-breaking third quarter ending December 1991, investor excitement moved CA's share price from under $7 to $17 in a matter of weeks—a clear recognition of the value of hard work over hype.

and the situation may change, but if it doesn't, it will be because CA is determined to keep spending on the production and selling of products, not image.

• A company with no clear rules is going to expend too much energy reinventing methods of operation. Yes, and a company with clear rules for the predictable is going to end up doing the wrong thing done the right way when the future turns out to be something other than the predicted.

• A company without a broad substratum of facilitators—what Charles calls a bureaucracy—will be constantly struggling to deal with its own bigness. Instead of making major decisions, senior managers may well get bogged down in thirty-dollar approvals. But the cost of such a bureaucracy is even heavier, both financially and operationally. That CA spends proportionately more on research and development than any other mature company is a function of its bare-bones administration: for every two secretaries it does not have, CA can hire one developer.

• A company that brings people up too fast is not going to breed seasoned managers, only brilliant ones, of which there may not be enough. Yes, but experience is much overrated; smarts, flexibility, and skill are the principal ingredients when tomorrow's problems no longer resemble today's. The twentieth-century emphasis on well-rounded managers has left us, predictably, without sharp ones to face the twenty-first.

• What about the problems of people working together whose personal relationships are so intense that business decisions may become personal? Business decisions have always been personal. Do we really want our business leadership to be composed of passionless automatons? We've got that now, the results of which are, alas, already in.

• Doesn't radical cost-cutting become counterproductive? Very quickly. In Brazil the controller of the São Paulo office was found to be sending an office boy out on the bus to make deliveries of software. To save on cab fare or a messenger service, unhappy clients were left hanging. A middle manager on Long Island patiently explained how he always telephones to make doubly sure a request from another manager at a branch office really requires overnight delivery: "Each one of these costs ten bucks." Right, and what about the calls, and his time, and the manager's time on the other end? Cost cutting can become counterproductive when it's in the hands of people who can't see a larger picture, who can't employ common sense. The solution is not to have those people around. Not controlling costs, however, calls for an entirely different solution. It is called Chapter Eleven.

In each of these situations, the plus stands out starkly against the minus and can be evaluated on its own terms and against the relentlessness of change and changing perspectives. There is a price for everything.

IV. Thrust

So when we ask if CA failed by not gaining market share in PC software, the short answer is yes, but the considered answer must be no: CA was involved in other things. To run after every opportunity is to commit to none. CA is probably in a better position to expand into PC software now than if it had tried to ride both horses five years ago. With durable multiyear cash flow (unlike PC software, data center programs are licensed and maintained over a period of years) and with so much experience in moving strong-product, weak-management companies into the black, CA now has the wherewithal to make a strong entry into PC software. If this happens, initially it will be through acquisition. Later, CA may well combine the better features of its PC programs with the features of mainframe programs and make them available on a variety of software and hardware platforms.

Will it happen? The process has actually been under way for some time and was recently formalized with the announcement of an ambitious blueprint of software integration—CA 90's—that, as it moves steadily from plan to implementation, will eventually establish CA as the kind of company that provides software solutions, not simply software products. This means that mainframe software will more and more be available for the PC, and PC software will be able to speak to mainframes. But it means something more: it is the first broad-scale plan of a system to isolate software components and make them modular, layered, Lego-like, connectable. CA 90's is today the world's most successful attempt to establish a standardization not of software but of its architecture. To comprehend this fully, we need to look back to the point in history where feet, inches, and yards became standard, interchangeable measurements, equally useful in the construction of dollhouses and cathedrals.

But this seriously oversimplifies the concept. CA's array of software is a collection of many products developed by highly eccentric individuals for many types of systems working on many types of hardware platforms. Defining commonality and isolating common elements to make each piece of software a subset usable with other building blocks is an approach that could scarcely have reached this point of development at any other company. And it is not only a matter of unparalleled technological genius.

It is a matter of style. Because whether he knows it or not, Charles Wang—once an undercapitalized entrepreneur looking for products and seeking the best way to develop or acquire them—is now building his products in emulation of the process by which he has built his company.

Look at the human process at CA. At its simplest level it is a mechanism to allow good people to connect with each other— with guidance but without hindrance—in order to produce more, better, quicker, and more profitably than single individuals serving a rigid structure. As an operating company, CA is thus a kind of internal market economy, endlessly responsive to pressures and interests from within and without. The type of people capable of dealing with the infinite adjustments of a universe of changing goals and shifting proportions are those people who are committed to working together and who are thus most skillful at working together. While they retain their quirks, desires, fears, loves, and preferences, they have committed themselves to a kind of human modularity. It is these people, individuals who have established working relationships of endless connectivity, who have now determined that software itself must have this endless connectivity too—or at least strive for it.

Here then is a process that is not going to show up in anyone's annual report. It cannot be numerically summarized under neat financial headings. It is composed solely of the subtle pulls and pushes of getting things right, then getting them better because yesterday's right won't work tomorrow.

V. Process

As a model, the CA process calls for such a completely radical approach that it would seem at first glance to be suitable only for new companies. Certainly, restructuring already established business entities into CA-type companies is not going to be easy: those strongly in the black should rightly be wary of drastic change, especially if they are public companies. Shareholders don't like tinkering with what works, and the dictatorship of the quarterly report in America leaves little room for slippage, even planned slippage. Companies in the red or heading toward it may not have a choice, though the failure rate is going to be high, if only because there is a significant difference between willing and able. A regimen of lean food and daily exercise is a preventative, not a cure. Sending a cardiac patient jogging is going to solve his problem rather too quickly.

Assume however that a company wishes to adopt CA principles in anticipation of the century before us. Can these principles be summarized? Only tentatively, because CA's first rule is that there are no rules. Its second rule is that there is a process. Its third rule is that the process is constantly changing.

But there is a logic to the process:

[1] Since all assets but one are commodities, and thus equally available to competitors, concentrate on the one asset that is unique: good people.

[2] The single most valuable characteristic of good people is trustworthiness. Technical skill, education, and experience may be liabilities in a world of rapid change. Skills can be learned; trust is character—it must be earned.

[3] Hire aggressive people chosen only by those to whom they will be responsible, and measure the performance of those responsible by results divided by manpower. The goal: better results with fewer people. The tool: better people.

[4] Zero-based thinking. Without reference to the past or current structure of the company, determine what it should be doing and what resources are necessary.

[5] On that premise reorganize the entire company as often as feasible but never less than once a year; reorg departments as necessary.

[6] Determine the best people for the most important positions by ranking employees against each other; promote from within.

[7] People fail for two reasons: lack of will and lack of skill. If the latter, the person may be in the wrong place. If the former, make the hard decision once—don't pass around the turkeys. When things go wrong, insist the person responsible understand why; if he learns, give him more authority.

[8] Ruthlessly prune nonperforming perks and status symbols. These hobble a constantly reorganizing company. Reward more authority with more cash. One good person at double the salary costs less than three deadheads and produces far more. Refuse to establish a salary structure; pay on performance.

[9] Talk through decisions in a group; make them individually on the basis of full responsibility. Let everyone manage something. A secretary who manages nothing gets to demonstrate

nothing—a loss to the company and to the individual. Managers should own products, not functions. A product-owner becomes responsible for the success of others; a function-owner, only for himself.

[10] Kill the roots of unproductive bureaucracy by abolishing standing committees and memos. Good individuals will seek collective advice when they need it. Don't waste everyone's time and effort turning doers into facilitators. Why? Because today really is the most important day of the most important month of the most important quarter of the most important year of your company's life.

Adhering to a vision, however, is rather more difficult than running down a list and nodding approval. That Charles and the company he has created have been true to their revolutionary vision is in fact the most unique thing about CA. One-shot success stories will always be with us, and there is a place for these in the history of capitalism. But industry is not creativity.

It is the effective harnessing of the creativity of many individuals to a common goal. Charles would shrug this off as "just good people." Charles: "Sure it's good people, because I make sure if they're not good people they don't work here—a bunch of crazies here to build a business." On a journey. Charles: "It's a journey, not a destination. God bless, we don't say, 'One billion, we'll retire.' We don't say, 'Two billion, we'll retire.' We don't say, 'Three billion, we'll retire.' It's a journey, not a place. As long as we're moving and the direction is right, then we're going to have a lot of fun and keep doing well. If you make a mistake, understand it and correct it. A billion dollars? Two billion dollars? They're just markers, signs on the road. So keep on going." Straight into a new century.